2026 LEVEL UP

100% UNOFFICIAL

BY GAMERS FOR GAMERS

SCHOLASTIC

IT'S LEVEL UP TIME!

Gaming accessibility has never been better, with cloud-save functionality and cross-platform progression becoming increasingly popular, allowing gamers to play however and whenever they like. And there have been improvements in designing games to be more accessible to as wide an audience as possible, with more games having options for high contrast mode visuals and audio descriptions. AI and VR are also having a moment, offering personalized experiences and pushing the boundaries of what's possible.

Level Up is your guide to the wide and wonderful world of gaming. Inside this book, we'll let you in on all the games you need to know about, why we love them, and how you can conquer them!

STAY SAFE AND HAVE FUN!

Games are wonderful, but you need to know how to stay safe while you're playing, especially when you're playing online. Follow these simple rules to have a great time!

1 Talk to your parents and agree on some rules about which games you can play, when you can play them, and whether you can play them online.

2 Never give out any personal information while you're gaming, including your real name, where you live, your parents' names, where you go to school, any passwords, or your phone number. Never agree to meet someone you've met online or through a game in person. As much as possible only play games with people you know IRL.

3 Tell your parents or a teacher if you come across something online that makes you feel uncomfortable.

4 Be nice to other players, even when you're competing against them. Don't say anything that might hurt someone's feelings or make them feel bad.

5 Take regular breaks when you're gaming. Give your eyes, hands, and brain a rest, and get your body moving.

6 Don't download, install, or stream any games without checking with your parents. Pay attention to the age ratings on games—they exist to protect you from content that might upset or disturb you, or that your parents won't be comfortable with you experiencing.

7 If you play mobile games outside, be aware of your surroundings. Don't play them alone and don't wander around the neighborhood without your friends or family.

2026 LEVEL UP

Writer:
Eddie Robson

Design, Editorial, and Project Management:
Dynamo Limited

ISBN 978-93-5954-296-6
Printed in India
at Nutech Print Services - India
This reprint edition, September 2025

CONTENTS

20

30

56

58

100

134

166

150

170

THE BIG GAMES

26 Bulwark: Falconeer Chronicles

200 Granblue Fantasy: Relink

Whatever games or types of game you love, we want to help you level up your gaming experience! Read on to get the scoop on the biggest games of the last twelve months, as well as the ones you might have missed (but will definitely want to know about!). Along the way, we'll share some interesting trivia and teach you the skills needed to take on a whole range of challenges. We'll also dive into the new console everyone's talking about: the Switch 2. Sound good? Great—let's go!

184 Sand Land

70 Pixelshire

80 Princess Peach: Showtime!

THE 30 GREATEST

GAMING MOMENTS

A snapshot of the world in games!

From the new Switch to the *Minecraft* movie, some of the biggest moments in gaming this year have been a long time coming—and others we never saw coming at all!

30

LONG TERM VISION Atari

■ Atari's big rival back in the day was Intellivision—search YouTube for "mr intellivision tv ads" to see how they thrashed each other in their adverts. Intellivision dropped out of the console wars in 1990, but it was revived as a retro brand a few years later, and in 2024 the brand was bought . . . by Atari. To anyone who grew up in the early 1980s, it's like hearing Sony bought Nintendo!

29

BIT PART PLAYERS Atari

■ Atari continued resurrecting their 1980s consoles, licensing retro games to produce modern versions that are a little easier to hook up to today's televisions. The cute Atari 400 Mini comes with twenty-five games built in, while the full-size replica 7800+ can actually play original cartridges, if your parents have any stashed in the attic!

28

COMING OF AGE
Mixtape

■ Ever wanted to step into a '90s teen movie? The innovative indie game *Mixtape* lets you do just that as it follows three young outsiders on their final day of school, having adventures on their way to a party—all set to a soundtrack of classic late 20th-century tunes. It shows games can tell any type of story!

27

WORLD BEATERS
Nintendo World Championships: NES Edition

■ Meanwhile you could take on the world retro style with *Nintendo World Championships: NES Edition*. This tribute to the famed 1990 event uses sections of thirteen classic NES games—including *Balloon Fight*, *Excitebike*, *Kid Icarus*, and the early *Mario*, *Zelda*, *Kirby*, and *Metroid* games—to create a series of speedrun challenges. With a local multiplayer mode, it makes a great party game and a new way into these 8-bit classics!

26

FIGHTING AROUND THE WORLD
Evo Championship Series

■ The Evo Championship Series celebrates its 30th anniversary in 2026. The event (it was called Battle by the Bay then) was founded to find the best *Street Fighter* player in the world, and it remains devoted to fighting games. Usually it's two events—one in Tokyo and one in Las Vegas—but in 2025, it's expanded to a third event in Paris!

25

A GAMES WITHOUT A GAME
Olympics

■ Old rivals *Mario* and *Sonic* costarred in the official tie-in game of 2008's Beijing Summer Olympics. The game was a huge hit, and a new edition became a fixture of the event every four years. But when Lee Cocker, a developer on the series, declared on social media that the International Olympic Committee (IOC) had declined to renew the license, and that there would be no Paris 2024 edition, there was an outcry! It wound up being the first Summer Olympics since 1988 to have no official console game.

24

OLYMPIC STANDARD
Olympics

■ The IOC seems more interested in bringing video games to the Olympics than in bringing the Olympics to video games. In 2024 they announced the Olympic Esports Series would be replaced by a full Olympic Esports Games, to be held every two years between the Summer and Winter Olympics. An Esports Games doesn't need as much preparation as a regular games, where large facilities need to be built—so the inaugural Esports Games have already been scheduled for 2027 in Saudi Arabia.

23

PARIS CATCH
Pokemon

■ We get the feeling *Pokémon Legends: Z-A* was originally meant to arrive in the summer of 2024, when the eyes of the world were on Paris for the Summer Olympics: It's entirely set in Lumiose City in the Kalos region, a location very much based on Paris. But there's no need to rush a game for the sake of a tie-in, and an all-urban *Pokémon* game is a very cool idea!

GO APE
Nintendo

■ The Universal Studios resort in Orlando opened Universal Epic Universe, which includes a Super Nintendo World. There are already Super Nintendo Worlds at the Universal Studios parks in Hollywood and Osaka, Japan. The Osaka and Orlando parks now include a Donkey Kong Country area!

22

21

MUSEUM PIECES
Nintendo

■ Kyoto was once the capital of Japan, and its history means it's full of tourist attractions. In 2024 another arrived—the Nintendo Museum! The company has been based in the city since it was founded, and the museum is built on the site it occupied in the pre–video game era, when it was a factory making hanafuda playing cards. You can discover that history at the museum and make your own cards, but also use giant Wiimotes or play Game & Watch games with your own shadow!

WHEELY GREAT Wheel World

■ Cycling has never translated that well to video games, so California studio Messhof took a totally different approach and brought us *Wheel World*, an adventure set in a funky cartoon open world, where you roam around looking for cycling races to take part in. Oh, and you need to prevent a looming disaster that threatens the world. Standard.

ALL FALL DOWN Atomfall

■ *Atomfall* gave us a British take on *Fallout*—an alternate-history game in which a real nuclear incident in the 1950s was much worse, irradiating much of the north of England. The player roams an uncannily detailed Lake District, encountering mutants, cults, rogue soldiers, and robots along the way!

18 CHIP TUNES Nintendo

■ Nintendo entered the streaming music world with a new app for Switch Online members. Nintendo Music allows you to stream the soundtracks of classic games from *Mario*, *Animal Crossing*, *Metroid*, and more—and it draws on your Switch play history to recommend music from games you like.

DIVE! DIVE! Subnautica 2

■ Innovative sci-fi survival game *Subnautica* got a sequel in 2025. *Subnautica 2* sees you once again stranded on an inhospitable ocean planet (very careless of you), and this time you can share the incredible sights and life-threatening stress with up to three friends thanks to a new multiplayer mode!

16

THE APPLE OF YOUR EYE Apple

■ The Apple Vision Pro, a new "mixed-reality" headset, launched in February 2024. While it can be used as a gaming device, its controls aren't as suited to games as the Meta Quest. Apple focused more on its potential for work and social use, as well as other types of media. *LEGO Builder's Journey* and *Soul Spire* are fun, but like all Apple devices, the Vision Pro is expensive, and hasn't been that popular.

15

GOING ROGUE
The Rogue Prince of Persia

■ Another roguelike game was planning an early-access release at the same time, and ended up delaying for a few weeks so it didn't get lost in all the fuss over *Hades II*. *The Rogue Prince of Persia* followed just months after the previous game in the series—*The Lost Crown*—and uses an awesome new comic book art style!

TO HADES AND BACK
Hades II

■ Dungeon crawler *Hades* was one of the surprise hits of recent years, and players were even more surprised when an early-access version of *Hades II* dropped in May 2024. This time you play as Zagreus's sister Melinoë, and it quickly got players just as hooked as the original!

TETRIS FOREVER

13

PAST MASTERS

■ Digital Eclipse is developing an interesting line in documentary/game hybrids. They launched their Gold Master Series with *The Making of Karateka* in 2023, combining a remaster of the game with interviews and material showing its development. They continued in 2024 with *Llamasoft: The Jeff Minter Story*, which presents an interactive timeline of the career of British designer Jeff Minter, including forty-two of his games, and *Tetris Forever*, telling the story of the legendary puzzle game. It's a fascinating way to present gaming history.

LONG HAUL FLIGHT
Microsoft Flight Simulator

■ Microsoft released the latest version of *Microsoft Flight Simulator* in November 2024, confirming its status as one of the longest-running game series of all time—and, in fact, it's Microsoft's longest-running software line. The first game came out in 1982, making it three years older than Microsoft Windows!

12

11

ASTRO-NOMMY
Astro Bot

■ The PS5 launched with *Astro's Playroom*, and Astro returned in 2024 with a new adventure, which established him as the cute mascot the PlayStation has always lacked. *Astro Bot* was up against *Final Fantasy VII Rebirth* at the Game Awards, with both games getting seven nominations—but *Astro Bot* took home four awards, including Game of the Year.

SONIC BOOM
Sonic 3

■ The *Sonic* movie franchise had a tricky start, with a dubious reaction to Sonic's appearance in the trailer for the first movie—and the film itself came out just as the COVID-19 pandemic was sweeping the world, limiting its run in cinemas. But with *Sonic 3* grossing more than either of the first two films, *Sonic* is now one of the most successful movie series based on a game—and a fourth film has been confirmed for 2027!

10

9

MOVIECRAFT Minecraft

■ The *Minecraft* movie was announced back in 2014, and a lot of us thought it would never happen. But ten years later a trailer finally dropped, set to the sound of the Beatles' "Magical Mystery Tour," announcing it was coming and it was *huge*. We'd all wondered how it would look—live-action or exactly like the game? They went for a blocky world with real textures, and sure enough it looks like *Minecraft* . . . but real!

8

BACK IN BLACK

■ *Minecraft* stars Jack Black as Steve, making this the third year in a row he'd appeared in a video game movie: He voiced Bowser in *The Super Mario Bros. Movie* in 2023, and Claptrap in *Borderlands* in 2024. Whereas *Mario* was by far the most successful video game movie ever made, *Borderlands*... was not. But you can't win 'em all.

7

PRO TIP
PS5 Pro

■ The downside of buying a console as soon as it comes out is there'll often be a tuned-up version a few years later. Sony has done this with previous versions of the PlayStation, so it was no surprise they released in November 2024 the PS5 Pro, with more storage space, upgraded graphics, and more processing power—and all in a smaller, lighter case. So if you're late to the PS5 party, at least you've got a more powerful console than those who bought it at launch!

BLANK VERSUS MultiVersus

■ Sadly, *MultiVersus* shut its servers in 2025. This free-to-play platform fighter featuring characters owned by Warner Bros. caused a huge buzz when it launched as an open beta in 2022, but then it was taken down for almost a year before coming back almost unchanged.

6

5

OLD SKOOL Fortnite

■ The moment *Fortnite* brought back its original map for a limited event in November 2023, it was obvious they'd have to make it a permanent thing. It's not that there haven't been great *Fortnite* maps with cool locations over the years, but there's just something about that Chapter 1 map. Plus, if you're not a fan of some of the gameplay elements that have been added over the years, *Fortnite OG* offers a simpler experience. (You can still sprint, slide, and mantle, though. No one wants to lose those, right?)

RAPID FIRE Fortnite

Fortnite launched perhaps its most ridiculous weapon yet. The Rap God Minigun doesn't just spit bullets, it also spits lyrics—specifically, the lyrics to Eminem's 2013 track "Rap God." You had to defeat Eminem himself to get it. It was soon vaulted, but we hope it makes a comeback.

3

EPIC SALE Epic Games

4

Disney has been working with Epic Games for years—that's how the *Fortnite* events involving Marvel and *Star Wars* characters came about—but in 2024 it got closer as Disney invested $1.5 billion in the company, getting a share of Epic in return. Expect more Epic-Disney collabs in the future!

2

HOLLOW PROMISES Hollow Knight: Silksong

Speculation over the Switch 2 launch titles led some to wonder if we'd finally see *Hollow Knight: Silksong*, originally scheduled for release in 2023. When the game's developers, Team Cherry, said no, it wouldn't be a Switch 2 launch game, one social media user pleaded with them to confirm the game was actually real. "Yes, the game is real, progressing, and will release," replied marketing manager Matthew Griffin confidently.

1

KART ON Nintendo

It was great to finally get the Switch 2 announcement, but there were no big surprises—and that includes the game that was running on the screen. No Nintendo system is complete without *Mario Kart*, and while *Mario Kart 8 Deluxe* is the bestselling game in the series, it's really just a spruced-up version of the Wii U's *Mario Kart* game, which came out over ten years ago. It's about time there was a new one!

MONSTER HUNTER WILDS

STEP OUTSIDE—IT'S A WILD, WILD WORLD OUT THERE!

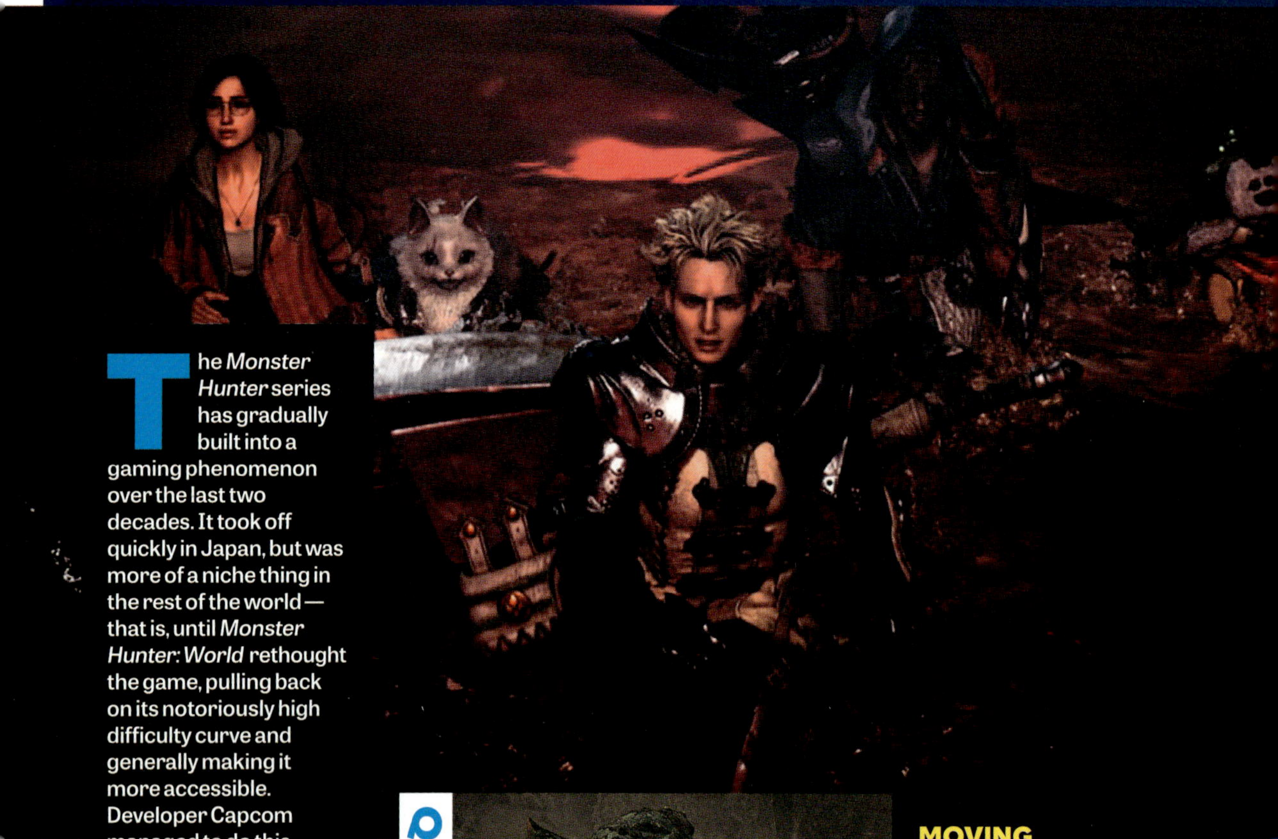

The *Monster Hunter* series has gradually built into a gaming phenomenon over the last two decades. It took off quickly in Japan, but was more of a niche thing in the rest of the world—that is, until *Monster Hunter: World* rethought the game, pulling back on its notoriously high difficulty curve and generally making it more accessible. Developer Capcom managed to do this while keeping the game challenging for the existing audience, and the result was a hit.

This means *Monster Hunter Wilds* is the most anticipated game in the series, and Capcom has taken their time with it, listening to players' responses to *World* and aiming to create a game that works for new players as well as longtime fans.

QUICK TIPS

MOVING INTO FOCUS

■ Hunting is transformed by the new Focus Mode. You can use this to target a monster's weak spots—so it rewards players for identifying what the weak spots are.

HIT THEM WHERE IT HURTS

■ You can also use Focus Mode to target an existing injury—so you can create a weak spot and then exploit it!

SHARP FOCUS

■ This also helps with accessibility, because it makes aiming and positioning easier. But also look out for weapons that have extra moves that only work in Focus Mode.

UNCHARTED TERRAIN

Wilds is based around a Guild expedition into the Forbidden Lands. A boy called Nata was rescued at the edge of this region, telling tales of a monster that attacked his village . . .

BREAKING NEW GROUND

One of the most notable changes in *World* was the removal of loading screens between zones, creating a seamless world for players to explore. *Wilds* goes further, removing loading screens when moving between a town and the wider region.

A NOSE FOR TROUBLE

There's a new type of mount, a Seikret, that gives access to new abilities. You can use its sense of smell to track automatically, which means you can do other things while on the move.

MULTITASKING

So, restoring health or sharpening your weapon is now possible while traveling. It also allows you to carry a secondary weapon, enabling you to adapt your hunting approach while in the field.

A RARE GEMMA

Even before the game's release, a new NPC became a huge hit with the fan base. Gemma, the wild-haired Research Commission Smithy, is your contact for crafting and upgrading armor and weapons.

FAST FACT

There has been a *Monster Hunter* movie, but you might not have realized. It went under the radar because it came out during the COVID-19 lockdowns.

LIKE THIS? TRY THIS:

TALES OF ARISE

This anime-styled RPG includes some truly epic monster battles with its bosses, the Gigant Zeugles. The *Tales* series is huge in Japan and has been running since the days of the SNES, but this is a great jumping-on point!

ORGANIC GAMEPLAY

The developers wanted to make the natural world of *Monster Hunter Wilds* behave like a real one, populated by monsters that behave like real wild animals rather than video game bosses. The result feels more detailed and immersive than any previous *Monster Hunter* game.

WHERE'D THEY GO?

Creatures in games can usually be found in a specific place, like an NPC who's always standing outside their house, regardless of the time of day. But in *Wilds*, monsters roam around, and that doesn't just happen randomly—it follows how real creatures act in the wild.

FOLLOW THE HERD

"It's not just, the carnivorous monsters go to a certain spot on the map to eat," said game director Yuya Tokuda. "If a carnivorous monster has become hungry and wants to get food it'll go attack and eat a herbivore, maybe attack it out of its herd. That'll cause its herd to scatter or move to a different place for safety."

CREEPED OUT

If you suffer from arachnophobia, *Monster Hunter Wilds* has a thoughtful accessibility feature. There's an option to replace all the spiderlike creatures with amorphous blobs, so you can actually play the game without freaking out! It follows similar options in games like *Star Wars Jedi: Survivor* and *Grounded*.

IN-DEPTH TRACKING

When you're hunting carnivores, remember they will be looking for herbivores to eat, so it might be easiest to find a herd of herbivores to get to their predator. Understanding these movements, and the life cycles of the creatures, is key to successful hunting.

FAST FACT

The Japan-only spin-off, *Monster Hunter Diary: Poka Poka Airou Village*, is a cute PSP game based around the Airou, the cat species of the *Monster Hunter: World*. This in turn inspired an anime series.

WEATHER THE STORM

Weather events have a greater impact on gameplay than ever before in *Monster Hunter Wilds*. For example, sandstorms lower visibility and unsettle wildlife. The apex predator of the desert becomes more powerful during storms, and a lightning strike will energize it even more! There's also a day/night cycle that changes creatures' behavior.

IT WON'T GROW BACK

Also, any changes to the environment persist. In other games, you might cut down a tree, leave the area, and come back the next day to find the tree has regenerated. None of that here! Your actions in this world have consequences, and it doesn't just quietly reset to default while you're not looking.

The Cub

A feral child is being hunted down—by golfers!

■ *The Cub* is part three of one of the oddest trilogies in video games. The first, *Golf Club: Nostalgia*, saw Martian colonists coming back to a ruined Earth to play a bit of golf. The prequel, *Highwater*, was a turn-based strategy game about a bunch of humans trying to escape the same world. Now Serbia-based developer Demagog Studio has brought us *The Cub*, a platform game inspired by *The Jungle Book*.

The Cub is a human left behind after the great exodus who has been raised by wolves. He's parkouring his way around when he's spotted by a group of Martians on a golfing trip who are also checking out the viability of Earth. Amazed by the Cub's survival, they start to hunt him…

FAST FACT

Igor Simić has also worked as a political cartoonist, which influences his satirical approach—the world of the trilogy is influenced by superrich tech bros trying to colonize Mars, and by Donald Trump's enthusiasm for golf.

Disney land

■ With *The Cub*, Demagog—led by visual artist Igor Simić—wanted to pay homage to the tricky platform games of the Sega Genesis era, and specifically games based on Disney movies like *Aladdin*, *The Lion King*, and *The Jungle Book*.

Beautiful ruins

■ As with previous games in Demagog's trilogy, the world is beautifully designed, and it's enjoyable just making your way through it and finding new areas. But don't get too caught up in it—it's not always easy to tell what's a platform and what's part of the backdrop!

Stay on your toes

■ Timing and reflexes are all-important—there are some tricky jumps and grabs, and distances aren't always easy to judge. On top of this, there's a stealth element—when the Martians appear, you must try to pass undetected.

The cub and the club

■ You don't have to have played the previous games to enjoy *The Cub*, but the narrative does overlap with the events of *Golf Club: Nostalgia*, so you'll get a bit extra out of it if you know the whole story.

Tune in

■ Radio Nostalgia, which featured in the earlier game, makes a comeback here. The Cub can receive via a helmet radio transmissions from Mars that fill in the backstory about the world generally and the Martians out looking for him.

INVECTOR: RHYTHM GALAXY

GROOVING INTO SPACE!

The rhythm-game craze of the 2000s, when gamers rushed out to buy massive controllers shaped like musical instruments so they could play *Guitar Hero* and *Rock Band*, is long behind us—but such games are still fixtures of the console world, and *Fortnite Festival* has introduced them to a new generation.

The 2019 game *AVICII Invector* had a cool visual concept—you steered a spaceship to the music of Swedish house DJ Avicii—and it gained an appreciative fan base. The follow-up, *Rhythm Galaxy*, partners with Warner Music to create a broader experience, with tracks by artists ranging from Charli XCX and Kojey Radical to Tina Turner and Duran Duran!

QUICK TIPS

GET INTO GEAR

■ Don't skip the calibration screens! The sound, picture, and inputs all need to be in sync for a rhythm game to work, so take the time to get them right.

FREE RIDES

■ While the campaign is important for unlocking all the songs, you may find a little practice in the free play mode is helpful when you get to the later stages.

GET IN LANE

■ The most important things to hit are the switches that move you between the lanes, so focus on getting those right above all else.

JOURNEYS IN SOUND

Invector: Rhythm Galaxy isn't just bopping for the sake of bopping. It has a light but sweet story, as a character called Ebula heads on an interstellar road trip with her friends Allisto, Atla, and Pollo in honor of her dead grandmother.

DROPPING TRACKS

The gameplay is the standard rhythm-game style, where notes come at you down the track and you hit the buttons with the best timing you can manage.

SECRET SONGS

Not all the songs are unlocked from the start. If your fave is one of the handful of locked ones, you may find this frustrating, but having to play through all the songs in the campaign adds to the sense of journey.

ONE NOTE

It has a Casual difficulty level—basically, a rhythm game for people without rhythm. This reduces the number of notes to hit, and you only need to press one button. The higher difficulties are tough!

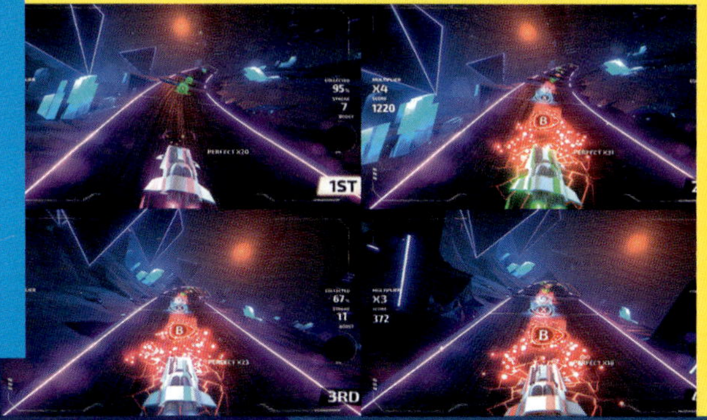

FORM A GROUP

There's also a split screen multiplayer mode, which allows you to play with up to three others. This is lots of fun, but we recommend everyone get a grip on the game on their own first!

FAST FACT

Invector: Rhythm Galaxy features the 2014 track by Charli XCX "Boom Clap," which previously featured in *Just Dance 2015*, *Just Dance Now*, *Let's Sing 2016*, and *Beatstar*.

LIKE THIS? TRY THIS:

HI-FI RUSH

A wannabe rock star finds his music player accidentally embedded in his chest, causing everyone around him to move to his soundtrack, in this game combining rhythm with action and RPG elements!

Bulwark: Falconeer **Chronicles**

Become the most chilled-out mayor!

■ *The Falconeer* came out in 2020 and was an aerial combat game with a difference: Instead of an airplane or spaceship, you controlled a giant bird. *Bulwark: Falconeer Chronicles* is set in the same fictional world, but it's a different game altogether—a city builder, where you must create a civilization in a wild landscape.

Developer Tomas Sala works mostly on his own. Maybe this is why his games are so individual. It may take a little while to get to grips with *Bulwark*, because it works differently from other games in its genre. It won't be for everyone, but it's worth checking out!

Simple style

■ A lot of modern city builders like *Cities: Skylines* are stuffed with micromanagement options, allowing you to get as deep into the details as you like. *Bulwark* isn't like that. You rock up at the rocks, place towers, and then connect them up.

FAST FACT

The third part of this trilogy, *Project: Ancient Waves*, will be "a seafaring adventure that plunges players onto the waves of the Ursee"—so across the three games, players will be able to explore this world in the air, on land, and under the sea.

Resources

You need resources to help your settlement grow. This is done by exploring in an airship. If you've got enough resources, you can click on parts of your city and develop them. It doesn't have the unlockable tech tree you find in most games of this type.

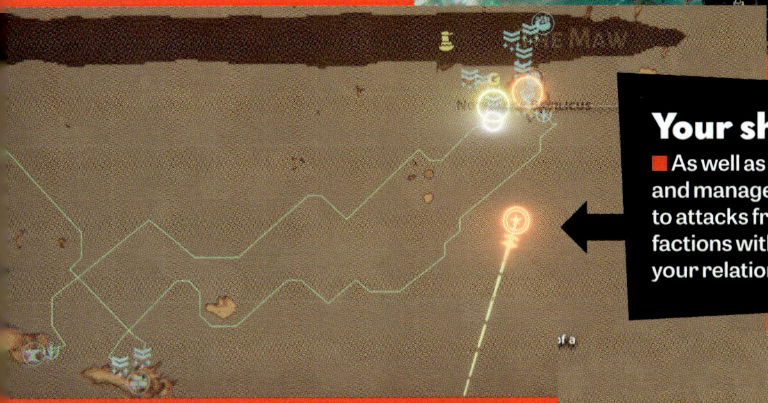

Your ship is coming in

As well as developing your city, you have to set up and manage a shipping network—which can fall victim to attacks from rivals and pirates. Your city also has factions within it, and whichever is strongest will affect your relations with other settlements.

On the campaign trail

There are three campaign scenarios, but none of them are that huge—you can get through them in a few hours. The free build mode lets you just go on creating. The whole game is intended to have the vibe of the early parts of city builders, before it all gets complicated.

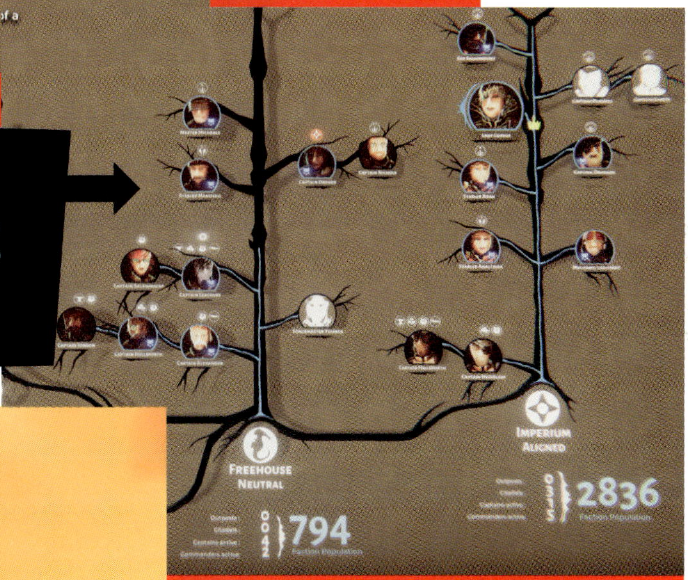

It's about the journey

In a way it's more like *Journey* (from 2012) than other city builders. It's not just about what you can do to affect the world, or even to "win" against the game—it's about immersing yourself in its landscape. Approach it with the right frame of mind, and it's very relaxing!

TEENAGE MUTANT NINJA TURTLES: MUTANTS UNLEASHED

No more hiding for the heroes in a half shell!

The Teenage Mutant Ninja Turtles have been popular characters in gaming ever since their cartoon series became a hit in the late 1980s—check out *The Cowabunga Collection*, which has thirteen *TMNT* games! But recently there's been a whole wave of new games featuring different versions of the Turtles—*Shredder's Revenge* is based on the original cartoon, while *Splintered Fate* is a *Hades*-inspired game with its own style—and now *Mutants Unleashed*, a direct sequel to 2023's *Mutant Mayhem* movie!

INTO THE LIGHT

Mutant Mayhem gave the Turtles a fresh new look, and *Mutants Unleashed* does a great job of translating this to a game. The world now knows about the existence of mutants, and the Turtles are trying to live alongside humans.

IT'S NOT ALL VIOLENCE

A lot of *TMNT* games have been straight beat 'em ups, but *Mutants Unleashed* is a light RPG. In between missions, you return to the sewer lair and use the XP you've earned to level up your skills.

WATCH THE CLOCK

Time is important in this game! You can't just wander around and do it at your own pace—the missions have deadlines you must hit. Early in the game, you have to focus on the current task. Later missions give you more time to talk to NPCs and train in the dojo.

SPREAD THE WORKLOAD

The game is especially fun if played with a friend—*TMNT* is all about teamwork and brotherhood, after all! It makes the game easier, though—and it's not that tricky to begin with!

PERSPECTIVE SHIFTS

The game lets you play each of the Turtles during the early missions, and you'll find they all play differently in combat. Later on, you can choose which to play on each mission and whether to focus your upgrades on one Turtle or spread across all.

FAST FACT

A game is in development based on yet another splinter (ha!) of the TMNT universe—the alternate-universe comic *The Last Ronin*, co-written by the Turtles' original co-creator, Kevin Eastman. In this, Michelangelo is the last surviving Turtle in a dystopian New York City!

Tales of the Shire: A The Lord of the Rings Game

Developing good Hobbits!

■ While the *Lord of the Rings* books are the definition of epic swords-and-sorcery fantasy, there's always been a cozy flip side to it all. The descriptions of the Shire, where the Hobbits live a blissful, relaxed existence of amusing riddles and second breakfasts, have fascinated many fans, and there are whole websites examining the Hobbit lifestyle.

Previous *Lord of the Rings* games have focused on fighting and quests—the types of thing video games are usually about. But with the rise of cozy gaming, the time is right for *Tales of the Shire*—a life sim where you create and customize your own Hobbit and then become a member of the Hobbit community!

By the way

■ *Tales of the Shire* is set in Bywater, which features in the novels as the site of the Battle of Bywater, the final battle in the War of the Ring. But there are no such battles here: At this point it hasn't yet become one of Hobbiton's official villages.

A hole lot of options

Hobbits live in Hobbit holes—homes set into the hillside, blending with the landscape. Players can customize their Hobbit hole to their heart's content—there's no grid, you can place your decorations and furnishings anywhere—and use it to store crops and flowers.

A meal good time

Food is central to Hobbit culture, and a lot of the activities in *Tales of the Shire* are based around food: farming, foraging, and fishing, as well as cooking. You can also host dinner parties or invite solitary guests as part of forging relationships with fellow Hobbits.

Well, that's wizard

You can also trade, go shopping—or just explore the world! Weather and seasons change as time passes, and there are different things to see at different times of year. You may even run into characters from the books!

Festival time

As with any life sim, you can unlock upgrades for things such as your skills, clothes, and home. But you also need Bywater itself to flourish, and your ultimate aim is to throw a superb Bywater Festival so the community can finally achieve village status!

ASTRO BOT

SONY'S MASCOT BECOMES A MAJOR PLATFORM PLAYER!

The PlayStation line has been Nintendo's main rival for three decades now, but Sony has struggled to create its own Mario—a mascot who stands for the creativity and history of the company. In fact, the last serious challenge to Nintendo on that score came in the early *Sonic* games.

Enter Astro Bot. He's previously appeared in two acclaimed games, *Astro Bot Rescue Mission* (2018) for the PS4's VR headset and the PS5 pack-in title *Astro's Playroom* (2020), which some felt was more a showcase for the PS5's power and features than a proper game. With *Astro Bot*, the character can now go toe-to-toe with Mario: It's a bigger and better game, and a great reason to buy a PS5!

QUICK TIPS

FREE BIRD
When you revisit it after completing a level, you can pay 200 coins to unlock the bird bot from its cage. This will help you locate all the collectables.

SAVE YOUR MONEY
Don't worry too much about spending your coin—it's not hard to come by and other than the bird bot, the main thing to spend it on is the Gatcha machine.

SAY CHEESE!
Check out the photo op stands, which will trigger cool in-game events when Astro Bot goes behind them and looks through the hole!

FEELING SCATTERED

The story of *Astro Bot* is that the little robo-guy's mothership has been blown up, scattering its pieces and crew across space, and he must search for them all.

FAMILIAR THEMES

In many ways it's the same as other platform games: You travel through six worlds with multiple sublevels. Each has different themes. You fight enemies and collect stuff. Pretty standard, right?

DOG GONE

However, it's also got lots of goofy twists on the usual elements—like the distance launcher, which is in the shape of a bulldog strapped to Astro Bot's back. All the designs are superbly cute.

FIND YOUR OWN WAY

The emphasis is on exploration and experimentation. Not everything in the game is explained—the fun is in figuring it out! It's only moderately challenging—this is an experience open to all players.

STEP IT UP

However, like most platform games, you need good reactions, judgment, and timing. If you want to test your skills, there are optional tougher levels as you get deeper into the game.

FAST FACT

If you haven't played *Astro's Playroom* since *Astro Bot* came out, fire it up—you'll find some new elements have been added, including four new bots you can rescue and transfer to *Astro Bot*.

LIKE THIS? TRY THIS:

SUPER MARIO GALAXY

The spacefaring collection quest of *Astro Bot* really reminds us of the *Galaxy* games—originally released on the Wii, you can get them on Switch as part of *Super Mario 3D All-Stars*.

THE VIP TREATMENT

A lot of the weapons are rubbish—make them better!

Astro Bot is bursting with references to PlayStation and its history, and of the three-hundred-plus lost bots you have to find, more than half are VIP bots, based on characters from classic PlayStation games. Some are playable in special levels based on their original games! Here's a few of our favorites and how to find them...

1

Security scouter

■ This is based on the Watcher from 2017's *Horizon Zero Dawn*. In the Feather Cluster: Machine Learning level, there's a pile of old computers inside an office building that can be accessed by a wooden bridge. The Scouter is hanging from a balloon above this. There are five other *Horizon Zero* bots in this level.

2

Gravity shifter

■ This is Kat from 2012's *Gravity Rush*. Find her in the Feather Cluster: Djinny of the Lamp level—you need to walk to the tail of the airplane (be careful!). This level also includes bots based on Raven from the same game and Jaster Rogue from *Rogue Galaxy* (2005).

Bonus bots

■ Other VIP bots include some based on characters from *Journey*, *Castlevania*, *SingStar*, *Space Channel 5*, and *LocoRoco*. More VIP bots based on games have been added since the game launch, along with extra content—these are free to anyone with the base game, and there are no microtransactions. Nice!

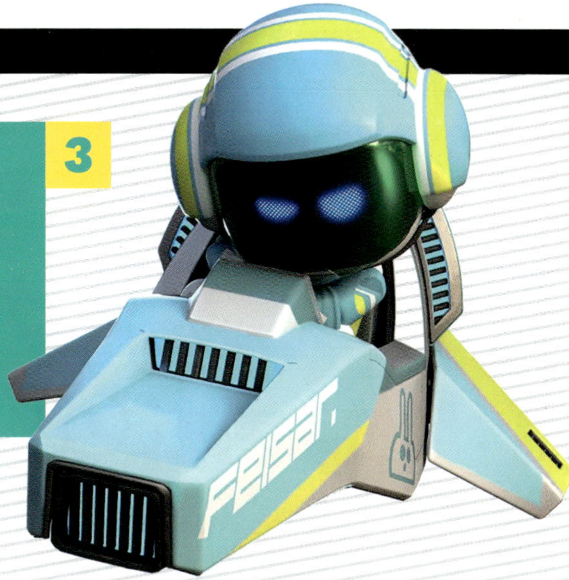

3 Future racer

■ The Feather Cluster: Orbital Blitz level includes four bots based on the 1996 PlayStation classic *Wipeout* and another from its sequel, *Wipeout 2097*. When you reach the circular passage with the three circular saw enemies, launch up through the glass and find Future Racer on the roof.

4 Vengeful spirit

■ This one's Jin from *Ghost of Tsushima* (2020). When playing Lost Galaxy: Danger Dojo, after obtaining the Western Warrior (William Adams from 2017's *Nioh*), drop down and enter the garden concealed behind the sliding panel to find Vengeful Spirit.

5 Dependable smuggler

■ This guy is Joel from *The Last of Us* (2013). In Tentacle System's Wormy Passage you need to look for two pillars, each with a cactus on top: Destroy those and use them to climb up to where there's another cactus that swells when you punch it. The Smuggler is inside. You can also find a bot based on Ellie.

FAST FACT

Team Asobi, the Sony-owned company that makes the *Astro Bot* games, was also behind the PS4's Playroom games, which were made up of augmented reality minigames designed to show off the console's camera and DualShock controller.

MARIO Roundup

Nintendo keeps finding new avenues for their most famous character!

MARIO & LUIGI: BROTHERSHIP

★ The *Mario & Luigi* series of RPGs originally appeared on Nintendo's handheld consoles, starting with *Mario & Luigi: Superstar Saga* on the Game Boy Advance in 2003. But the developer that made them, AlphaDream, was shut down in 2019, and the series seemed to have ended with the fifth game, 2015's *Paper Jam* on the 3DS.

However, Nintendo has revived the series for the Switch. *Brothership* has been developed by Acquire, best known for their ninja and samurai games, but it's quite different from those! It sees Mario and Luigi crossing the seas of Concordia on a vessel called Shipshape Island—it's a cross between an island and a ship (that's where the title comes from, you see).

QUICK TIPS

GET IT TOGETHER

★ Like previous games in the series, *Brothership* uses turn-based combat. You have to combine Mario's and Luigi's attacks to win these battles using rhythmic hammer-bashing and jumping—but you also need to be ready to defend.

FIGHT SMARTER

★ Luigi Logic is an important part of exploration, but you can also use it in combat. If you can reach a certain point when fighting a boss, Luigi might notice something that will turn the battle your way!

PLUG IN

★ You'll discover Battle Plugs as you go along. These can do things like automate healing and protect you from elemental damage—but the real depth comes when you combine plugs for different effects.

UNCHARTED WATERS

★ The lands of Concordia are fragmented, and Mario and Luigi must bring them back together! Along the way they face off against enemies who look remarkably like electrical plugs of different types.

A WIDER SCOPE

★ Navigation on Shipshape Island is done via telescope, but the telescope is also a cannon, which shoots Mario and Luigi to their destination. The artwork does a cool job of taking the cartoony style of previous *Mario & Luigi* games into a 3D world.

CHECK IT SNOUT

★ You'll never be left unsure what to do next, thanks to your companion Snoutlet, who'll explain your objective as you arrive at each new place. (Be warned, there's quite a lot of dialogue in this game!)

LOOK FOR LOGIC

★ Sometimes, when there doesn't seem to be a way forward, the answer will occur to Luigi. These moments are Luigi Logic, and will lead to a puzzle or minigame that will help you progress.

MAKE CONNECTIONS

★ Once you've completed the quests on an island, you can connect it to Shipshape Island and take it with you. This means that, while traveling, you can revisit those lands and find new things!

FAST FACT

Before *Brothership* came out, the bestselling game in the *Mario & Luigi* series was the 2009 DS game *Bowser's Inside Story*, which sold 4.56 million copies.

LIKE THIS? TRY THIS:

MARIO & LUIGI: SUPERSTAR SAGA

★ The game that started off the series sees the brothers venturing into the Beanbean Kingdom to find the stolen voice of Peach. It's great, and you can find it in Switch Online's Game Boy Advance library.

SUPER MARIO PARTY JAMBOREE

★ This is the thirteenth game in the *Mario Party* series (or twelfth, if you count *Mario Party Superstars* as a compilation rather than a new game, or sixteenth if you count all the handheld ones . . . Whatever, they've made a lot of these games!). Nintendo promised this would be the biggest *Mario Party* game yet, and it has delivered: 112 minigames is the most any game in the series has had.

However, Nintendo has also managed to recapture what made the best games in this series so good, as most fans felt the Wii and Wii U games weren't up to the same standard. The first Switch game in the series, *Super Mario Party*, was a step in the right direction and *Superstars* tapped into the classics, but *Jamboree* finally gives the Switch a great new *Mario Party* game!

QUICK TIPS

NINJI MOVES

★ There are two unlockable characters. The first, Ninji, is on an island just beyond the Rhythm Kitchen. Get in the balloon above Party Plaza, swivel the camera around, and look out for two islands. Ninji is on the slightly bigger one.

BAY AREA

★ The other unlockable character is Pauline, mayor of New Donk City, who Mario had to rescue in his first game, *Donkey Kong*. Like Ninji, she's easy to unlock—find her on a tiny island left of Minigame Bay.

GO PRO

★ Pro Rules is a great new setting where skill is much more important than luck—but you'll need to complete a game on any board before you can use it. This also unlocks the Vote for Minigames option.

GAME ON!

★ **There's a single-player campaign, and it's OK, but really *Mario Party* is all about the multiplayer action. If you've played and enjoyed a game in the series before, you'll find something to love here!**

BY THE BOARD

★ *Jamboree* offers a choice of seven boards—five new ones plus the return of Mario's Rainbow Castle from the original *Mario Party* and Western Land from *Mario Party 2*. These classic boards must be unlocked, however.

PASS THE MOTION

★ Most of the minigames use motion controls, but to make the game more accessible, you can turn these off and use buttons instead. There's a nice mix of random chance and skill in the selection of games.

TWENTY'S PLENTY

★ Online play has also been improved, including a twenty-player online mode called the Koopathlon where players can race against one another. Watch out for the Bowser round, which sends losers back several spaces!

BEATS AND BEETS

★ There are several side modes. The standout of these is Rhythm Kitchen, where players compete in culinary-themed rhythm games by shaking the Joy-Cons to the beat. It's a neat extra and definitely worth checking out!

FAST FACT

***Super Mario Party* and *Mario Party Superstars* sold more copies than the first ten home console *Mario Party* games put together—and both sold more than the previous bestseller, *Mario Party DS*.**

LIKE THIS? TRY THIS:

OVERCOOKED: ALL YOU CAN EAT

★ This compiles both the *Overcooked* games, which are frantic co-op games set in a busy kitchen. They can get very chaotic and you may lose your temper with friends and family, but they're some of the best couch co-op games around!

PAPER MARIO: THE THOUSAND-YEAR DOOR

★ Nintendo has been treating its back catalog well in recent years, with excellent Switch remasters of games like *Link's Awakening*, *Metroid Prime*, and *Super Mario RPG*. The second game in the *Paper Mario* series is a particularly good candidate for a revamp, because it came out a few years into the life of the GameCube, which was not one of Nintendo's more popular consoles. It got great reviews, and many rate it as one of the best *Mario* games of any type—but it sold fewer copies than the original game. The remaster adds a few things, but mostly doesn't mess with it—just polishes the graphics and sound so it can shine as the classic it always was. With *Brothership* bringing the *Mario & Luigi* line back, it's a great time for *Mario* RPGs!

QUICK TIPS

IMPORTANT POINTS

★ When leveling up, go for Flower Points first, then Badge Points. One upgrade to Heart Points is useful, but otherwise you can leave it until later, when battles get tougher.

TAKE A SHOT

★ Some parts of the scenery can be opened up with the right character or power-up—like cracks or peeling back walls. If you can't open them yet, take a screenshot to help you remember where it is.

GO THE WHOLE HOG

★ The first badge to buy from Dazzle when you get the chance is the Item Hog badge. This raises the chances of getting items from defeated enemies.

CRYSTAL CLEAR

★ **Like many RPGs, *The Thousand-Year Door* is a collection quest. Peach asks Mario to help her find the treasure behind the fabled Thousand-Year Door—but then she's kidnapped. Mario must locate the seven Crystal Stars that open the door.**

GOOD ON PAPER

★ This remaster doesn't change the 2D paper cut-out style of the original—it just makes everything sharper, and it's a really beautiful game. There are some tweaks to gameplay, including the fast travel system and Mario's item and coin capacity.

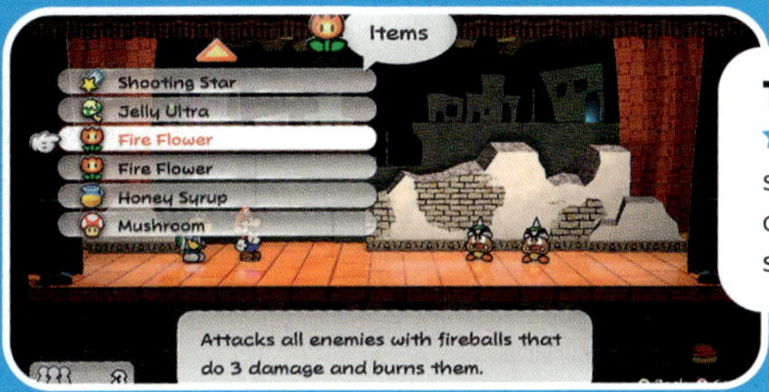

TAKE YOUR TURN

★ Combat is turn-based in classic RPG style, and it's a smart move to think about the order of your party before combat begins. You may be able to use one character to set up an attack by another.

WHAT'S HAPPENING, BROTHER?

★ There are lots of very funny touches in this game. Always speak to Luigi when you get the chance—you'll find he's off on a peculiar adventure of his own . . .

INTO THE FOLD

★ Mario's paper form isn't just cosmetic! He has a number of origami transformations, activated when he's on the correct panel. He can become a rolling tube, a boat, a plane—or just turn sideways to slip through gaps.

FAST FACT

The soundtrack has been completely rerecorded, but there's an option to play with the original music—you just need the Nostalgic Tunes badge, available from Lovely Howz of Badges in Rogueport.

LIKE THIS? TRY THIS:

SUPER MARIO RPG

★ *The Thousand-Year Door* sits very nicely alongside this remaster of the very first *Mario* RPG—a much-loved game, which survives the update with all its goofy humor intact.

TRANSFORMERS: GALACTIC TRIALS

THE ROBOTS HIT THE CIRCUIT!

Transformers has been going for more than forty years, and for nearly all that time there have been games based on these robots that can change into cars, planes, and such. So why has it taken so long for someone to make a racing/combat hybrid where you can switch between vehicle and robot modes? Now that they've done it, it seems so obvious.

Galactic Trials isn't perfect—the control system in the shooting sections needs a bit of work, and the story is so contrived they may as well not have bothered giving it one—but it's great to see a game that uses what makes *Transformers* unique.

QUICK TIPS

GET OVER THE LINE
Don't forget this is a race with fighting, not a fight with racing! If you get too distracted by fighting your rivals, it could cost you the win.

GET BUFF
The Prime Relics are equippable modifiers and give you buffs. You can choose which you want to use before a race, so think about what you need most for a particular circuit.

GET THE DRIFT
As with *Mario Kart* and games like it, drifting is an important skill to master. The longer you drift, the more boost you get—but watch out as it drains your health bar!

WHY ARE WE FIGHTING?

Galactic Trials has a plot, of sorts: The Transformers are racing to decide who gets to keep the Prime Relics that have been stolen by Nemesis Prime (the evil clone of Optimus Prime, obviously). It doesn't make a lot of sense, but we're here for the racing and the shooting and that's what we get!

OLD-SCHOOL STYLE

The look of this game is really cool. The Transformers themselves are nicely chunky, looking like their original selves rather than the movie versions, and all the neon adds to the 1980s vibe.

LEAGUE OF LEGENDS

There's a good range of characters—as well as Optimus, the roster includes Soundwave, Shockwave, Megatron, Arcee, and Bumblebee, and you unlock more as you play. It's a little odd that Autobots end up fighting Autobots at times, though!

CHANGE IT UP

At various points in the race, the participants transform, and the action changes to shoot-'em-up. This can favor players who are lagging behind, as the ones in front are the ones who get shot at the most!

ON TRIAL

The course design is also good, and as well as the standard Galactic Trials mode, you can just go for straight racing. The racing is in the style of arcade games and *Mario Kart*, with power-ups to collect.

FAST FACT

***Transformers* was created by Japanese and American toy companies, but the first *Transformers* game was made in the UK in 1986 by Ocean Software, for the Sinclair Spectrum and Commodore 64.**

LIKE THIS? TRY THIS:

TRANSFORMERS: DEVASTATION

Maybe the best of all *Transformers* games, *Devastation* goes for a clean, first-generation style and relentless action in the vein of *Bayonetta* (both games were made by the same studio, PlatinumGames).

Destiny 2: The Final Shape

How does the last chapter shape up?

Space-based FPS *Destiny* has developed into one of gaming's great epics. The original came out in 2014, and after four expansions for that game, developer Bungie released *Destiny 2* in 2017. Since then, the base game of *Destiny 2* was made free-to-play, while hardcore players became hooked on a series of expansions that continued the story and deepened the lore. Bungie promised this story would have a proper ending, and in 2024—marking ten years of the series—they delivered *The Final Shape*. If you've stuck with it all this time, your faith has been rewarded!

Stay on your guard

In the sprawl of updates and expansions, the lore of *Destiny* has become pretty complicated, and it can be daunting for newbies. But broadly speaking, it's a tale of the Guardians, spacefaring warriors who are battling the forces of evil.

Get in shape

But what is the Final Shape? Is it this *massive* triangle? Nope—it actually refers to the final state of the universe, which the forces of Darkness are trying to bring about. There's some debate about what that state is, but the Witness—the villain behind all this—has his own idea.

Hands up

Weird sci-fi imagery has always been a strong element of *Destiny*, and as the game gets closer to the heart of evil, the universe gets stranger and more disturbing. The Pale Heart of the Traveler is a space where thoughts and emotions can change reality.

New tricks

For a game that's had this many expansions, it's surprising how many new mechanics they've come up with for *Destiny 2*'s final chapter. You'll find yourself increasingly juggling combat and puzzles and learning new moves along the way.

FAST FACT

A free-to-play mobile game, *Destiny: Rising*, is on the way. It takes place in an alternate timeline, shortly after the collapse of civilization: "a new generation of Lightbearers, resurrected by mysterious entities known as Ghosts, set out to restore humanity's prominence and secure its future," developer NetEase said.

The end?

Adding more chapters to a story is always easier than ending it, and asking questions is easier than answering them. Some players wondered if the nature of the big bad behind all this would ever be revealed—but *The Final Shape* does give a satisfying payoff!

DRAGON BALL: SPARKING! ZERO

REIGNITING A BRIGHT SPARK!

Back in the days of the PlayStation 2, the main series of *Dragon Ball* games was *Budokai Tenkaichi*, which in Japan went by the title *Sparking!* There were three of these arena fighting games, which later came to the Wii, and many still rate them among the best of the many *Dragon Ball* games (and there have been loads—we think about seventy-five, but we keep losing count—many of them only released in Japan).

Now it's back, and called *Sparking!* everywhere rather than just in Japan. It's been given the subtitle *Zero* because it's designed as a game anyone can get into, whether they're a long-term fan or have just got into it with the new *Dragon Ball Daima* anime.

QUICK TIPS

KI FACTS

Ki charging is a major part of this game. Hold down the right trigger to charge—but be ready with the right shoulder button, which blocks your opponent's Ki blasts.

DISENGAGE

Taking cover behind the scenery can be the smartest thing to do! You can charge your Ki, and opponents will often waste energy blasting through to you.

HIT 'EM UP

Be careful not to waste your charged attacks. Use a melee attack first to soften up your opponent and make sure that charged attack hits. You'll get better combo damage this way, too.

A FAITHFUL FEEL

Before the *Sparking!* series, *Dragon Ball* fighting games used a side-on 2D style, like *Street Fighter* and *Tekken*. *Sparking!* used a 3D view that felt more like battles in the anime. This was what made those games so cool, and they've recaptured it well in *Sparking! Zero*.

FLYING FISTS

Mastering this game is less about executing tricky special moves and more about coping with the chaos in the 3D arena. There's a lot to think about, and it's all moving fast.

KEEP YOUR COOL

Don't worry if you find it difficult at first—it's got a pretty steep learning curve. It helps if you have an anime brain, and are used to following insane action!

PLOT BEATS

In story mode, you choose from eight fighters and enter the main arcs of *Dragon Ball Z* and *Dragon Ball Super*—but you're not trapped into playing through the same old familiar story!

FLIP THE SCRIPT

The path of the narrative can change depending on the player's actions, sending you into a Sparking Episode. Stick to established *Dragon Ball* lore if you prefer—but if you want to freshen it up, take a different path!

FAST FACT

Akira Toriyama, the creator of *Dragon Ball* and one of the most important manga artists of all time, sadly passed away in 2024. He also did character designs for video game RPGs including *Dragon Quest* and *Chrono Trigger*.

LIKE THIS? TRY THIS:

DRAGON BALL FIGHTERZ

Not just one of the best *Dragon Ball* games, but one of the best manga/anime games full stop: a fighting game that, unusually, has a great single-player mode rather than being all about the multiplayer.

THE TOP TIER

One of the most appealing parts of *Sparking! Zero* is its huge roster of characters. There are 182 in all (including nineteen versions of Goku), and 110 are unlocked from the start. Here are our picks for the best five in the game.

GOKU (SUPER) ULTRA INSTINCT

This form of Goku has good stats but also two great moves—No Backing Down, which sends him straight into Sparking! Mode, and Ultra Movement, which gives you a dodge and a counterattack. He's got a high DP cost, though. He can be unlocked at the shop for 120,000 Zeni after completing the Goku's Mentor mission.

SUPER SAIYAN ROSÉ

In DP fights, you have a limited number of Destruction Points, stopping you from making a team of all the strongest fighters. The regular form of Goku Black has a middling cost of 5 DP, but with skill points you can transform him into the more powerful Super Saiyan Rosé (who usually costs 8 DP). This gives you a very strong fighter fairly cheaply.

FAST FACT

***Dragon Ball* is the fifth bestselling manga of all time—impressive when you consider it has fewer volumes than any of the series above it on the list!**

YAJIROBE

Not the toughest character by a long way, but Yajirobe can be a strategic pick for your party because he costs just 2 DP and is hard to knock down. Get enough skill points and you can unlock his heal ability, which makes him a very frustrating opponent. He can be purchased from the shop for 30,000 Zeni after completing Vegeta's Secret Maneuver.

SUPER VEGITO

Super Vegito's Afterimage Strike is an awesome move, making him near-invincible for a short time. He's also unlocked from the start of the game, so he can be a good one for new players to get to grips with.

GOGETA (GT) SUPER SAIYAN 4

Overpowered? Maybe! The Super Saiyan 4 form of Gogeta has the ability to switch quickly to Sparking! Mode, and his Wild Sense is a great evasive move. On top of this, his normal attacks are super fast. You can buy him for 120,000 Zeni after hitting level 10 and completing the Zen Oh's order task of fighting as Gogeta ten times.

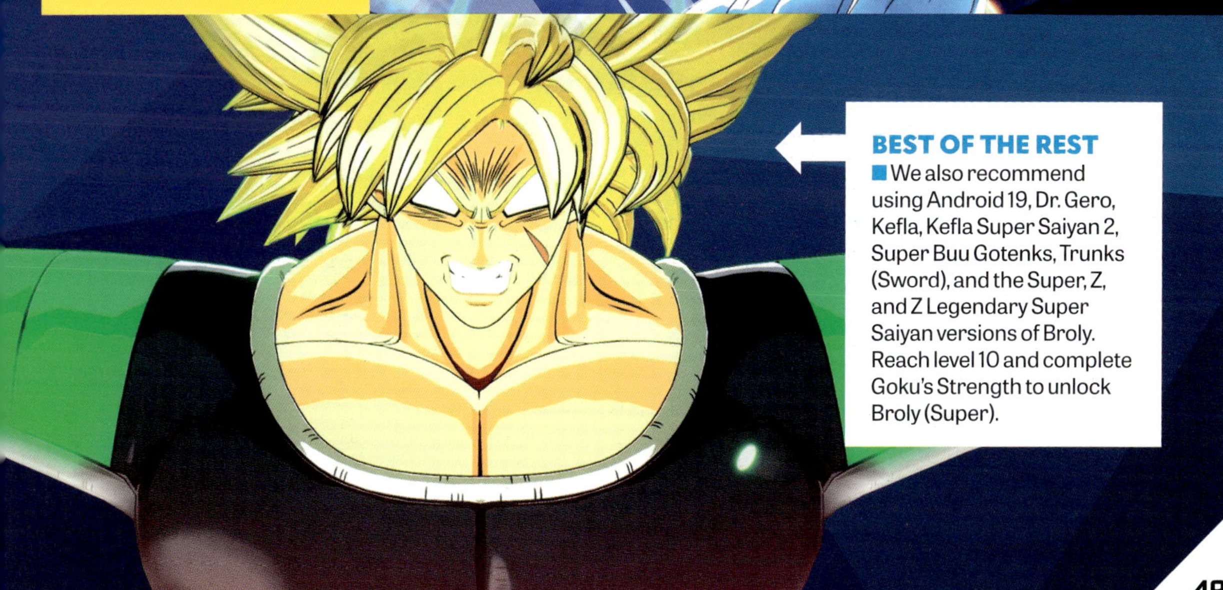

BEST OF THE REST

We also recommend using Android 19, Dr. Gero, Kefla, Kefla Super Saiyan 2, Super Buu Gotenks, Trunks (Sword), and the Super, Z, and Z Legendary Super Saiyan versions of Broly. Reach level 10 and complete Goku's Strength to unlock Broly (Super).

SUPER MONKEY BALL BANANA RUMBLE

HAVE A BALL AND GO BANANAS!

In the early 2000s, Sega took the basic gameplay of the 1984 arcade hit *Marble Madness* and, in a genius move, replaced the marbles with monkeys in oversize hamster balls, which the player had to guide around a game area to the goal. *Monkey Ball* was born, and for ten years it was everywhere, on every platform, an endless parade of rolling monkeys. The early games were fearsomely addictive, but after a while the quality tailed off.

For over a decade there were no new *Monkey Ball* games, just a few remasters of old ones. But now the series is back with *Banana Rumble*! It won't surprise anyone who's familiar with previous games—but it's tons of fun!

QUICK TIPS

TAKE FLIGHT

When you want to tackle speed challenges, YanYan is the fastest of the starters—though she's also very light, so often flies into the air, and has poor braking.

TAKE A TURN

Baby is also quick and has great braking. Meanwhile Doctor has the most powerful spin, which makes him good at getting around obstacles. Palette combines speed and spin.

TAKE IT SLOW

Different characters are better suited to different stages. AiAi is an all-arounder. For steep slopes and narrow paths, a slow character with good braking—like MeeMee or GonGon—is best.

ROYAL RUMBLE

Single-player mode offers one hundred stages to play through. When you've completed them, you'll unlock one hundred EX stages! All the unlockables, should keep you occupied for a long time.

MISSION CREEP

Even when you've cleared the entire game, there are missions to go back for, like collecting a certain number of bananas before making it to the goal. This is where the real challenge lies!

READY TO RUMBLE

The game also offers multiplayer battle options, which bring in sixteen players in online play and up to four in local multiplayer. But we think the pure puzzle joy of the single-player mode is best!

GOTTA DASH

And that's not the only inspiration this game takes from *Sonic*. There's a new Spin Dash move, which is handy to get you moving, and could give you the edge in multiplayer races!

PERFECT PASS

You can also purchase a Sega Pass that lets you play as the core *Sonic the Hedgehog* characters, as well as Axel from *Crazy Taxi* and Beat from *Jet Set Radio*.

FAST FACT

The original *Monkey Ball* arcade cabinet had a joystick shaped like a banana! The checker pattern ground is similar to the special stages in Sega's *Sonic 3 & Knuckles*.

LIKE THIS? TRY THIS:

SUPER MONKEY BALL BANANA MANIA

This marked twenty years of *Monkey Ball*, and is essentially a remaster of *Super Monkey Ball Deluxe*, which compiled all the levels from the first two games and added some more. It's still the ultimate *Monkey Ball* experience!

SUPER MONKEY BALL BANANA RUMBLE—UNLOCKABLES GUIDE

Expand the game as you play!

There are over three hundred cosmetic items to unlock as you play through *Banana Rumble*, so those of you who love to customize your character will find plenty of reason to keep playing and playing! There are also five unlockable characters...

FAST FACT

Gamer Thomas Tilley made a custom controller out of a model AiAi, a plastic ball, and a mouse trackpad so he can play *Monkey Ball* by actually moving a monkey ball. Check it out on YouTube!

1

Tee

Three art thieves called the Gala Family are planning on stealing OOPArts (Out-of-Place Artifacts), and you'll meet them at the Rose Garden. While they seem like bad guys at first, later you'll find they're willing to help you—and when you clear world 7, Candy Castle, they're unlocked. Tee has a fast-charging Spin Dash and braking, but is a little weak in other areas.

2

Fes

Fes, the second of the group of thieves, also has a fast-charging Spin Dash, but it's difficult to control due to her lack of braking. Other than that, she's a good all-arounder with a little more in weight, and she controls smoothly. None of this gang has fewer than two stars in any category.

3

Dr Bad-Boon

Dr Bad-Boon is an evil baboon (bad-boon, get it?) and the villain of *Super Monkey Ball 2. Banana Rumble* is his debut as a playable character. He's actually the easiest to unlock—you just need to play one online Battle Mode match!

4

Easel

Easel, Palette's dad and a notorious art thief, has been taken over by the OOPArts curse. This curse is lifted after you clear world 10 in Adventure Mode, and he appears for purchase in the shop. His more powerful Spin Dash comes with a cost, as its charging speed is slower.

5

Val

Val, the last of the Gala Family, has a very powerful Spin Dash, but its cooldown is longer. He also has high weight and spin, which makes him useful when you really need to stay on the ground. All of the unlockable characters can be bought at the shop for 3,000 points.

More unlockables

Once you complete the initial one hundred levels and hit the EX worlds, you'll find even more clothing to unlock. The first seven EX worlds all have super-EXclusive unlockable items of clothing, while the last three EX worlds have special themed balls!

TOP 10 CAT GAMES

Even dog people love feline like a cat in these games!

A *lot* of recent games have a main character who's a cat. We're not sure why, but who cares—cats are awesome. Whether you want to look after virtual cats or play as a pirate cat on a quest for treasure, there's a game for you here!

10 Cat Slide Tiles

In this cute puzzle game, you must slide the tiles around to make a path for the cat—it's like those toys you've probably seen where you have to get all the pieces in place to make a picture. If you find the right arrangement, the cat will be able to step through and collect the keys needed to unlock the next stage. But watch out—some of the pieces are red herrings, and you can waste a lot of time trying to fit a piece you don't even need!

AVAILABLE ON:
Nintendo Switch, PS 4, Xbox Series S/X, Xbox One, PC

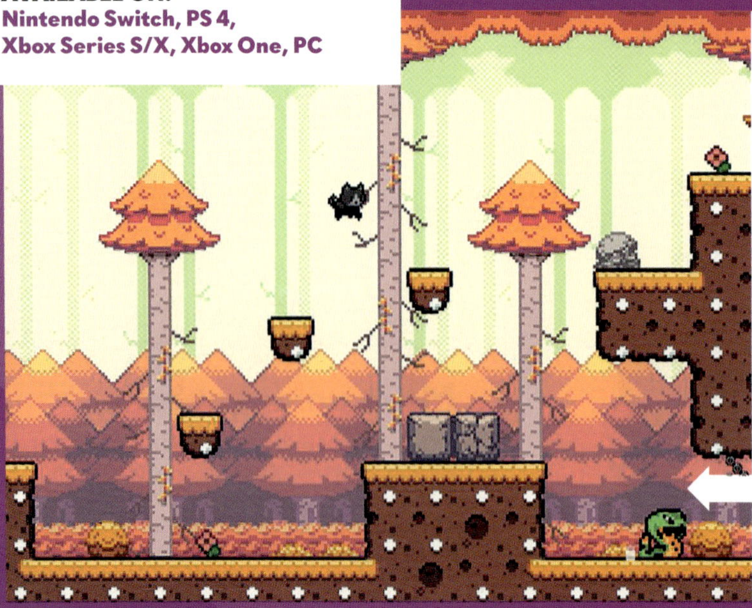

09 Neko Rescue Tale

This may look cute, but it reflects the reality of cats: They're hunters. The main character is on a quest to find their friend, but must progress through levels filled with creatures, pouncing and swiping them to death. You'd be alarmed if your cat brought this many birds and rodents home in one day, that's for sure!

AVAILABLE ON:
Nintendo Switch, PS5, PS4, Xbox Series S/X, Xbox One, PC

08 Sissa's Path

■ This one's a puzzle game in the *Sokoban* genre (named after a game called *Sokoban* from 1982, where you push boxes around a warehouse—find it for free online; it's addictive and quite tricky). You move a cube-shaped kitten called Sissa around a board, pushing balls of wool into position: Get them all in place to clear the level. It's a great game of its type, and having a cute cat is a nice bonus.

AVAILABLE ON:
Nintendo Switch, PS5, PS4, Xbox Series S/X, Xbox One, PC

07 Cattails

■ It's a life sim in the style of *Stardew Valley*, but it's about cats. There are rival gangs all competing for territory, and you can earn XP by fighting challengers as they rock up. You can level up your hunting, swimming, and foraging skills, and you can also develop your relationships with other cats! This makes it sound like there's a lot of drama, but like a lot of these cat games, it's a relaxed experience.

AVAILABLE ON:
Nintendo Switch, PC, Mac, Linux

06 Cat Souls

■ An original take on classic platform games, *Cat Souls* gives its cat hero seven lives (we thought nine was the traditional number, but whatever) and something unusual to do with them: When a life is used up, it becomes a platform with which you can access new areas. It's a neat idea, meaning if you find a jump particularly tricky, you can get a platform to help you cross it. The pixel art is lively and its creative touches help it stand out from the indie retro crowd.

AVAILABLE ON: Nintendo Switch, PS5, PS4, Xbox Series S/X, Xbox One, PC, Linux

05 Peace Island

■ A fascinating project in open-access development on Steam, *Peace Island* sees nine cats in a remote Maine island community waking up to realize their humans have gone. From there it's a mystery game as the cats try to discover why this happened, how they might bring the humans back—and if they want to bring them back at all! It's a fascinating world, with lots of depth for the cats to discover!

AVAILABLE ON: PC

04 Cat Rescue Story

■ This started life as a mobile game, and like most mobile games it's pretty simple—but it works surprisingly well on consoles. Unlike the other games here, this simulates the experience of actually looking after cats: You inherit a house and decide to turn it into a cat shelter. You take in cats, give them whatever medical attention they need, feed them, play with them (taking control of each cat in a minigame), and then find them a new home—earning rewards that upgrade your shelter in the style of tycoon games. It's unchallenging, but very wholesome and pleasant.

AVAILABLE ON: Nintendo Switch, PS 4, Xbox Series S/X, Xbox One, Android, iOS

03 Little Kitty, Big City

■ More cozy vibes from this adventure game in which a cat gets lost in a large Japanese city. The ultimate aim is to get back to your owner's apartment, but there's lots to explore along the way—you can chase birds, climb into trash cans, and generally do the stuff cats do. It's even got fast travel (hopping into the sewers and popping up from a manhole) and a leveling-up system: If you eat tuna, you increase your ability to climb ivy. You must eat all the fish to be able to reach the apartment!

AVAILABLE ON: Nintendo Switch, Xbox Series S/X, Xbox One, PC, GeForce Now

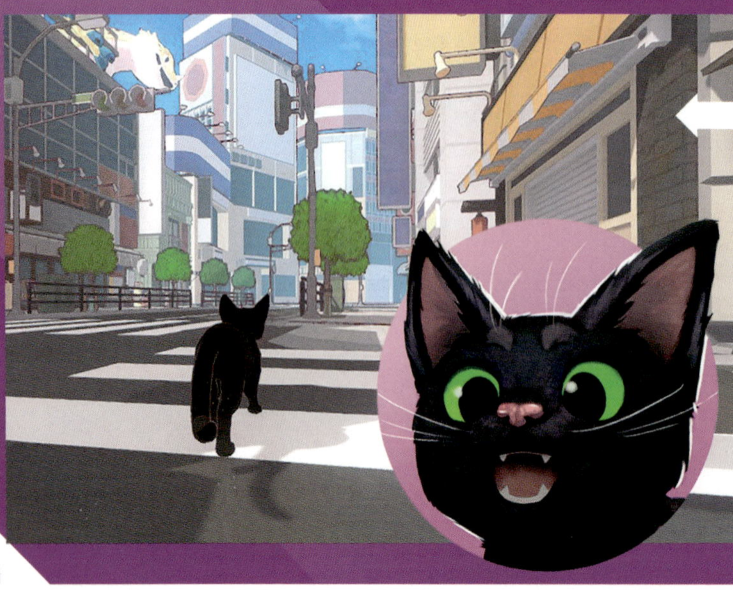

02 Stray

■ Like *Little Kitty, Big City*, but sci-fi. A stray cat falls into a futuristic underground city that's been abandoned by humans, and is now inhabited by their robot servants. With the help of a drone, the cat—controlled by the player—makes their way to the surface, avoiding security drones and mutant bacteria. It's a great idea, and there's so much fun to be had in opening up pathways by acting like a cat—knocking stuff over, pawing at things, and getting inside them. There are open areas where you can just wander around like a real stray and enjoy the exceptional level design, but you'll also want to uncover the story of what happened here.

AVAILABLE ON: **Nintendo Switch, PS5, PS4, Xbox Series S/X, Xbox One, PC, Mac**

01 Cat Quest III

■ The *Cat Quest* series of action RPGs have been running since 2017. The first in the series took place in the open world of Felingard, while the second required you to control cat and dog characters in co-operative gameplay. The third sensibly gets rid of the dog but keeps the co-op mode, and it's easily the best one yet. This time it's a pirate quest in the Purribean, as you see the North Star that will grant wishes to its holder (bit of a *One Piece* vibe there). It's not a huge game, but if you find the massive hundred-hour open worlds of some RPGs daunting, the cleverly designed world of *Cat Quest III* is perfect for you. Great writing and characters make this one of the most enjoyable indie games of recent years.

AVAILABLE ON: **Nintendo Switch, PS5, PS4, Xbox Series S/X, Xbox One, PC, GeForce Now**

THE LEGEND OF ZELDA: ECHOES OF WISDOM

FINALLY, SHE'S NOT JUST THE LEGEND—SHE'S THE STAR!

It took 38 years, but here it is at last—a *Legend of Zelda* game where Zelda is the main playable character! Nintendo surprised everyone with this game—*Tears of the Kingdom* had taken so long, no one expected a new *Zelda* title for a while, but *Echoes of Wisdom* was announced at Nintendo Direct in June 2024 and released three months later.

Echoes of Wisdom is closer to the series' 2D roots, using a similar graphics style to the Switch remake of the Game Boy classic *Link's Awakening*. In fact, *Echoes* started out as an expansion of the *Link's Awakening* dungeon editor before becoming a game in its own right—and it was going to star Link, but Nintendo's development team decided switching to Zelda might prepare players for its very different gameplay style…

QUICK TIPS

FAIRY GOOD

■ When you get the option to go to Gerudo Desert or Jabul Waters, tackle instead the rift at Stilled Lake Hylia, northeast of Lueburry's House. This unlocks the Great Fairy Fountain where you can buy more accessory slots!

IT'S ALWAYS RIGHT TO FIGHT

■ You can always collect more Swordfighter energy, so go into Swordfighter form whenever you need to. Return to Lueburry's House after every dungeon to upgrade those abilities.

MIGHT BE SOMETHING IN IT

■ Like the Korok Seeds in *Tears of the Kingdom*, an oddly positioned rock or bush can be a sign there's a Might Crystal hidden under it.

RIFTING AWAY

You start off *Echoes of Wisdom* playing as Link, but soon he falls into one of the rifts that have appeared all over Hyrule. Zelda is imprisoned by an imposter posing as the King, but a fairy called Tri helps her escape and gives her a powerful magical totem—the Tri Rod.

ECHO LOCATION

The major difference between *Echoes of Wisdom* and previous *Zelda* games is it's not based around combat! Instead, the gameplay is guided by Zelda's ability to create "echoes"—copies of things she finds in the world.

IMAGINE THAT

The building functions in *Tears of the Kingdom* let players make objects the developers hadn't thought of, and there's a similar flexibility to *Echoes of Wisdom*. Anything you've found in your efforts can be used to tackle obstacles!

COPY AND PASTE

Only certain things can be copied with the Tri Rod, but once the pattern has been learned, Zelda can use it at any time. So while the game looks and plays very differently from *Tears of the Kingdom*, they both encourage creativity.

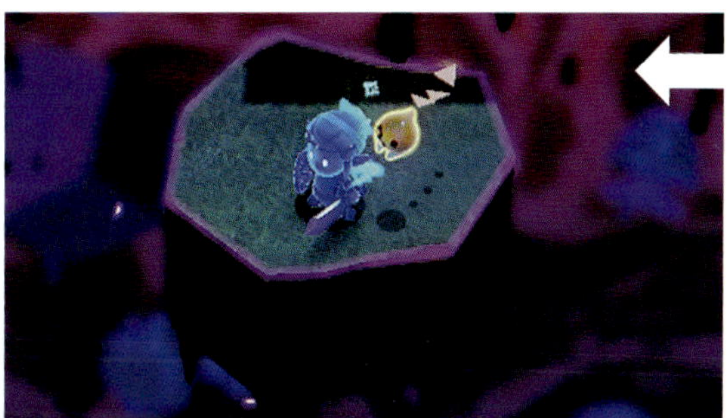

MAKING MINIONS

Zelda can transform into Swordfighter form—but this drains energy, so she can only battle for a limited time. However, after defeating creatures, she can produce echoes of them to battle for her.

FAST FACT

Zelda starred in two games released on the Philips CD-i in the '90s, which didn't use the *Legend of Zelda* brand—*Zelda: The Wand of Gamelon* and *Zelda's Adventure*. The latter is considered one of the worst games ever made!

LIKE THIS? TRY THIS:

THE LEGEND OF ZELDA: SPIRIT TRACKS

The DS *Zelda* games are tricky to adapt for Switch because of how they use the touchscreen on the DS. This is a shame as it means *Spirit Tracks*, in which Zelda adventures alongside Link, has fallen by the wayside—but it's worth checking out!

THE ESSENTIAL ECHOES IN ECHOES OF WISDOM

Helping you make sound decisions in Hyrule.

There are 127 echoes to collect in *Echoes of Wisdom*. Some are obvious, others need a bit of work to uncover—but here are five we think you absolutely need. Remember, if you find the pop-up echoes menu clunky, you can always hit the plus button to open the notebook view.

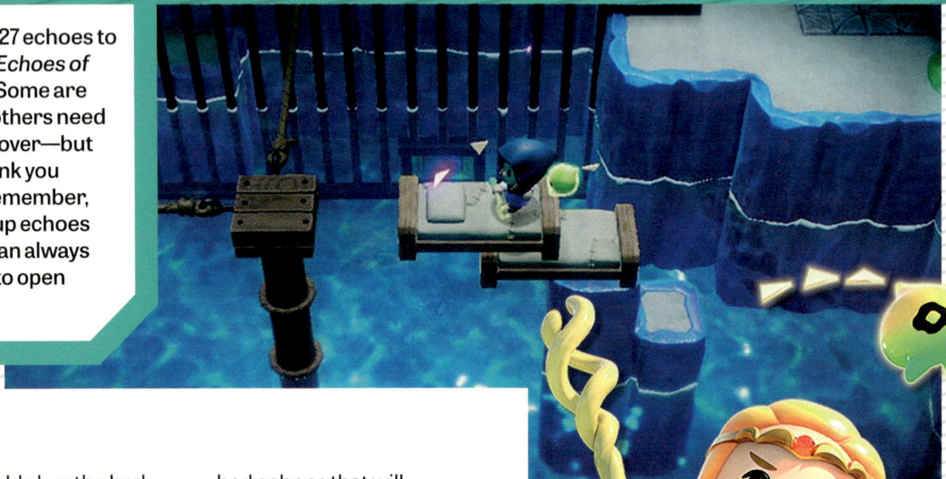

1 Bed

Once Zelda has the bed echo, she can create one whenever she needs to rest and recover health. They're also very handy building blocks! You can collect better bed echoes that will regenerate health faster, but you should still carry smoothies, not just for quick heart refills but for all the other benefits they give.

2 Platboom

These appear in a cave in the Stilled Desert Temple Ruins, and it might seem like all you can do is dash past them like *Mario* Thwomps. But by using Bind and creating a Sand Piranha to attack one, you can destroy it and collect its echo—which makes it much easier to complete this area!

Flying Tile

When you're able to enter Gerudo Sanctum, you quickly reach a fast travel point. In the room to the left of this chamber you'll be attacked by flying tiles. While dodging them, it's easy to miss that you can learn their echo. You won't *believe* how useful it is for crossing large gaps.

3

4

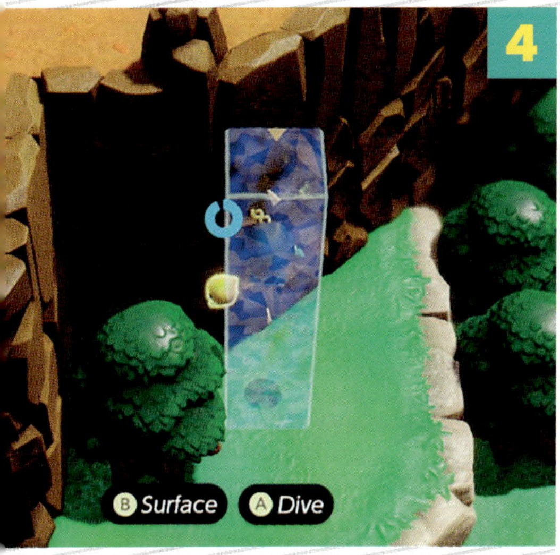

Water Block

It's better to tackle Gerudo Desert before Jabul Waters, but once you go to the latter you'll find something even better for vertical travel—the water blocks stack easily and allow you to create towers of water you can swim through upward. The Bombfish echo is also a great one to pick up!

Finest Fighters

When creating creatures to fight for you, the higher their cost, the more powerful they are. The best are the Boomerang Boarblin (level 2), found in the western Gerudo Desert, that has ranged attacks; the Freezard, with its ice powers; the annoying teleporting Wizzrobe; and the most powerful echo in the game, the Lynel.

5

Crow

These can be found everywhere when you reach Hyrule Field, so they're easy to get, but they have a benefit that's not immediately obvious. Their first hit on an enemy gets you a burst of Rupees, so they're great for farming cash: They're also good for distracting enemies while you get on with doing other stuff.

FAST FACT

The year 2026 marks the 40th anniversary of *Zelda*! The original game was released in Japan on February 21, 1986, and could only be played with the Family Computer Disk System add-on for the NES.

Sid Meier's Civilization VII

A game for the ages!

The *Civilization* series has been running since 1991. It was an attempt to combine city-sim games with tycoon games, plus elements of the board game Risk. It became the leading example of "4X" strategy games, where the player aims to eXplore the land, eXpand their empire, eXploit the resources, and eXterminate the opposition.

The particular strength of *Civilization* is the way it lets you select your own approach: You start with a small, primitive village, and you can try to achieve domination by military might, economic power, scientific strength, or cultural sway. The sixth game in the series came out in 2016, so it's been away awhile—but what has this one added to the classic formula?

Dividing your time

In previous *Civilization* games, time just stretched on continuously as long as you kept playing. *Civilization VII* makes a big change, with time being divided into Ages. These are like chapters of your story, with cliffhangers at the end of each Age.

FAST FACT

Designer Sid Meier's name was added to *Civilization* to distinguish it from an earlier board game with the same title—he's since had his name in other titles like *Sid Meier's SimGolf* and *Sid Meier's Pirates*!

Foundation stones

In the earliest Age, the Age of Antiquity, you pick one of over a dozen civilizations from the ancient world. This sees you developing your foundation—your cities, your technology, and your relationships with other civilizations.

Under new leadership

The game also remixes history in new ways. Previously a real-life leader would be attached to the country they actually led, but now you can choose to put them in charge of any civilization. Catherine the Great of Russia can be the Empress of Rome!

A changing world

You'll find that during an Age, there are limits on what you can do, so you can't just use the same tactics for the entire game. This makes the whole experience feel more structured than previous *Civilization* games, with more of a narrative.

Beyond the sea

In the Age of Exploration, your civilization changes into a whole new one from another era! In this segment you head out across the oceans and try to conquer or colonize other nations as you see fit.

FABLEDOM

ONCE UPON A TIME, THERE WAS A CITY-BUILDING GAME . . .

Fabledom is based on a simple and appealing concept: It's a city-builder set in a fairy-tale world. And while medieval city-building games tend to have combat and strategy elements, this game does things differently: It's also a dating sim.

Your character is a prince or princess whose family has sent you to a newly discovered continent to learn about ruling a kingdom while also looking for someone to marry. And you don't just get a ready-made kingdom—you have to found it yourself. As your city expands, you'll meet eligible rulers of other lands and try to make a good match. It's quite different from other types of dating sims, because the future of your kingdom depends on it!

QUICK TIPS

GET INN!

■ The simplest way to boost happiness is to build an inn: They're relatively low-cost and high-impact. Make sure they're in the middle of an area, covering the highest possible number of homes.

HUMAN RESOURCES

■ Move your workers around, because early in the game you probably won't have enough to run everything at once. And definitely don't keep workers on your farms in winter, when farms won't be operating.

PLOT IT OUT

■ You don't need to use 3x3 plots for houses—they look good but there's no real benefit. The 2x2 plots are cheaper and prevent everything getting too spread out.

PRINCE-IPAL CHARACTERS

Remember we said your family has packed you off here to learn about kingdom management? Well, you're not the only one! All the local rulers are young princes and princesses, just like you.

CHECKING THE VIBE

This isn't just about dating, it's also about diplomacy! You'll find that different rulers will be impressed by different things. Some can be bought with money; others respect strength more. Your relationship affects how you interact with them.

TAKE YOUR TIME, OR ALL AT ONCE?

There are two different options for how to play *Fabledom*: You can have a more guided experience, where you unlock new things at different levels, or you can have a more sandbox-y game where everything is available from the start.

COURTLY LOVE

You need to gather and unlock resources in order to be able to send courting gifts to other rulers. Once you've chosen who to send your gift to, a new set of quests opens up around that character.

TELLING TALES

Sometimes you'll come across an element of a well-known fairy tale, like Cinderella's slipper or Jack's beanstalk. These open up fun side quests.

FAST FACT

***Fabledom* is the first release from Grenaa Games, a development studio that's based in Sweden and is made up of just two people.**

LIKE THIS? TRY THIS:

MANOR LORDS

If you want to try a medieval city-builder with a more realistic approach, *Manor Lords* has combat and strategy elements. By the time it entered early access on Steam, more than three million users had it on their wish lists!

FOUNDATIONAL ADVICE IN FABLEDOM

Take confident first steps into your new kingdom!

One of the annoying parts of any city-builder is when you make a mistake and have to tear buildings down so you can do it again, but properly. It can be daunting building your first city in a new game, so here are some pointers to help you avoid getting things wrong and make sure you survive your first winter!

1 Keep the neighborhood clean

■ Your initial plot of land isn't that big, and expansion costs money, so plan your settlement carefully. As in *SimCity*, people don't like living near heavy industry like stonemasons, and this will lower the desirability of an area. If happiness drops below 60 percent, people won't come to live there.

2 On your feet

■ Put farms in between your housing and industry, but make sure you don't put the housing and industry *too* far apart. With no cars, buses, or subways, your subjects will be walking to work, and the farther they have to travel, the lower their efficiency becomes.

FAST FACT

Other fairy tale-inspired games include the visual novel *Cinders*, which flips *Cinderella*, the beautiful RPG *Child of Light*, and the light adventure game *Fairy Tale Mysteries 2: The Beanstalk*.

3 Content farms

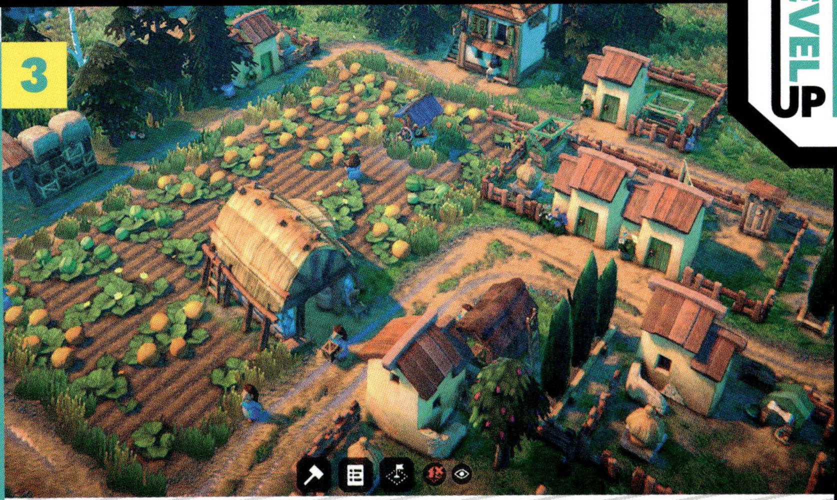

■ Food supply is *very* important. Start by building some medium-sized farms (around forty tiles) devoted to vegetables, which are cheap to grow. Each home has sub-buildings—by default these will be random, but you can deselect that and choose food-producing buildings like greenhouses and chicken coops. These are less desirable, *but* they're a great way to boost food production.

4 Get well soon

■ The game is set in a simpler world than ours, so there's less to think about in terms of plumbing, power lines, and public transport. But your residents will need water, so you need to make sure every home has access to a well. Leave spaces for them as you build.

Time for heroes

■ The people in *Fabledom* feel more like characters than the people in other city-builders. For instance, when you place Hero Quarters, you get a hero who can deal with things for you, including randomly spawning monsters and other oddities. You don't have to kill these creatures—they may have benefits, such as a talking tree that enhances wood production!

5 According to plan

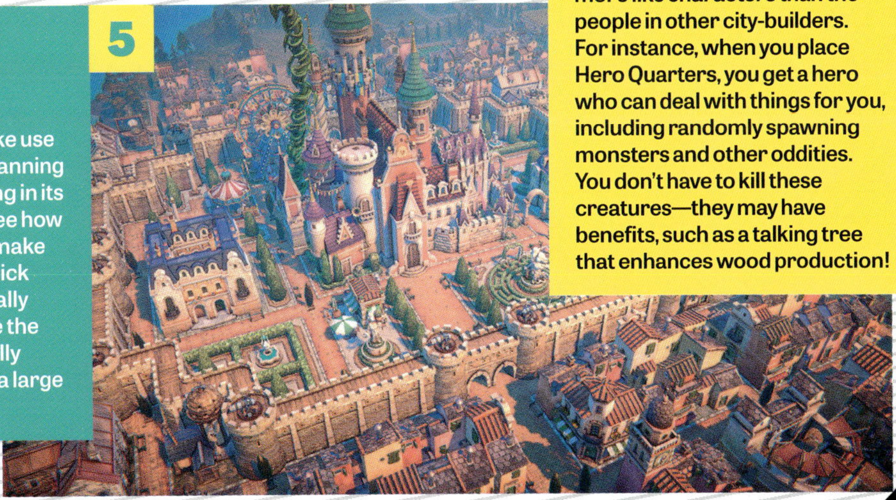

■ As you develop, make use of the game's great planning mode to get everything in its right place. You can see how it'll all look when you make a plan, then you can click on each piece to actually build it when you have the resources. This is really useful when building a large new district.

LEGO HORIZON ADVENTURES

The robot apocalypse in brick form!

The *Horizon Zero Dawn* games are RPGs set in a 31st-century world overrun by machines. Sounds like an obvious choice for a LEGO® game, right? No? Well, they made one anyway, and it's pretty cool! It's a sort-of remake of the first game in the series, moved into a LEGO® world and with less emphasis on the whole apocalypse thing. The developers aimed to make a game that's accessible to newcomers and gamers of all ages!

COMMITMENT TO THE BRICK

■ Some LEGO® games just design the characters and the main interactive elements in LEGO style, but in *Horizon Adventures*, everything you see is LEGO. "So even though they're made as digital assets," narrative director James Windeler says, "you could build them technically out of physical sets."

SHORT AND SWEET

The story can be completed in about ten hours, and achieving 100-percent completion takes around twenty hours. Anyone who has played the original will enjoy spotting references to it!

FAST FACT

The inspiration for *LEGO Horizon Adventures* came partly from how developer Guerrilla Games designed the dinosaurs for the original game using DUPLO® blocks!

CHANGE IT UP

There are lots of customization options for Aloy herself and the hub world, and this is the coolest part of the game. If you complete levels and tasks at the hub, you unlock costumes and building elements—and the community board will give tasks where you need to dress up in specific outfits.

SAME OLD STORY

As with the original game, the protagonist is Aloy, cast out from her tribe as a baby, who has undergone combat training and picked up a handy AR device to enhance her senses. The AR device is called Focus, and—as in the original game—it's an essential part of combat. It highlights weak spots on enemies, enabling Aloy to target them and deal extra damage. The game has five difficulty settings, making it easy for anyone to enjoy.

CRYPT CUSTODIAN

ALL HIS NINE LIVES ARE USED UP . . .

We couldn't decide whether to put this in our Top 10 Cat Games (see pages 54–57) or Top 10 Metroidvania Games (see pages 188–191), so we gave it a spread of its own! *Crypt Custodian* was created by Metroidvania specialist Kyle Thompson, and it sees you take the role of Pluto, a dead cat who's been unfairly sentenced to become a janitor in the afterlife. As Pluto undertakes a series of puzzles, dungeon crawls, and boss fights, he talks to the dead and learns there may be treasure that will help him contact the living. If you've been looking for something that gives you the same hit as *Hollow Knight*, look no further!

QUICK TIPS

TAKE IT EASY

■ You can change the difficulty at any time, so if you're struggling to get past a tricky boss, you always have the option of making it easier (unless you're already on the easiest setting).

JUMP TO IT

■ The dodge roll is a great move, but it has a brief cooldown. Sometimes jumping is the better option, especially if combined with an attack.

FLOOR IN YOUR REASONING

■ The floor lights puzzle in Neon Crest is solved by starting at the bottom left corner, going right, then up, then left—then connecting the rest by working your way around.

JUDGMENT DAY

Pluto has led a good life. But in the process of getting to Kendra, who runs the afterlife, he can't help but break some of her statues. (They're in the way!) This causes him to be banished…

GOING UP TOP

While the gameplay is classic Metroidvania—move around the map, gathering power-ups and keys enabling you to unlock new areas—it uses an overhead view like the early *Zelda* games rather than sideways scrolling action.

IT'S A JOURNEY

It takes around twelve hours to play through *Crypt Custodian*—but its world is large and richly detailed, with so much to discover. It's also surprisingly emotional in the way *Spiritfarer* was.

TALK TO THE DEAD

The story is superb—speaking to the other banished souls who gather at The Sinner's Inn is great fun—and the quirky visuals mean it's always enjoyable to play. Currency is earned by cleaning up piles of grime, which is a nice touch.

BOSSING IT

The combat is really sharp, too, and often quite challenging. Dodging is essential, and so is making use of the various wearable upgrades and special attacks you pick up on the way. Best of all are the frantic boss fights!

FAST FACT

Kyle Thompson's brother Eric makes all the music for his games. The *Crypt Custodian* soundtrack is on streaming services, while his music for *Sheepo* is on Steam.

LIKE THIS? TRY THIS:

ISLETS

Kyle Thompson's previous game was one of the indie hits of 2022. *Islets* is a very charming and wholesome adventure that sees you connecting a series of floating islands but also connecting their people by talking to them.

THE BIG SWITCH UP

WE'RE FINALLY GETTING OUR HANDS ON NINTENDO'S NEW CONSOLE!

The Switch has had an unusually long lifespan. Nintendo, Sony, and Microsoft usually leave about six years between console launches, but the Switch was Nintendo's leading model for more than eight years—a mark of just how successful it was.

Nintendo also held back from launching the Switch 2 because they wanted to avoid the situation that happened with the PS5 and the Xbox S/X, where shortages of components meant the consoles constantly sold out, and scalpers who got a hold of them were able to make huge profits selling them. But it's finally here!

MORE OF THE SAME?

After months of rumors and leaks, Nintendo released a video of the Switch 2 on January 16, 2025. Several times Nintendo has surprised everyone with a fresh take on what a games console can be . . . but not this time. It's not a console you can wear like a shoe or anything like that!

The Switch 2 is another hybrid console with a dock and detachable wireless controllers, and no one really expected them to do anything different. The original Switch works perfectly for the people who love it, and any major changes would risk moving the design further away from something that works brilliantly well.

SO WHAT'S DIFFERENT?

The Switch 2 is a little larger than the Switch, which means a larger built-in screen.

There's now a USB port at the top.

The button layout is basically the same, but with one extra button on the right, and the shoulder buttons are larger.

The Joy-Cons don't slide into place but are held on magnetically. You can clip them into a grip to form a separate controller, same as with the Switch.

The built-in stand on the back is U-shaped for greater stability and can be adjusted to different heights.

A LINK TO THE PAST

The best thing about the Switch 2 is that it's backward compatible with the Switch, so you can play your collection of Switch games on the new console. With the PS5 and Xbox S/X also going for backward compatibility, it seems this is the future of gaming. Just as people don't want to get their old phone out to use their old apps, they want to keep their old games on their new console.

Nintendo can't guarantee every game will work on the new system, but the majority of games will—so the Switch 2 benefits from one of the best and biggest libraries any console has ever had, totaling over 12,000 games!

HISTORY REPEATING?

The Switch is a hard act to follow, for sure. It's very close to being the bestselling console Nintendo have ever made: Its 146 million sales fall just short of the incredible 154 million units shifted by the DS. (Both are behind the PlayStation 2, which sold 160 million units.) More importantly, it comfortably outsold the PS4 and the Xbox One to become the biggest console of its generation.

Nintendo has been here before. After the GameCube sold disappointingly, they came up with the Wii, a console designed to appeal to a different audience than the one Sony and Microsoft were targeting. It was a hit, and they followed it with the Wii U, which . . . wasn't. Players weren't thrilled by its touchscreen GamePad, and the Wii U lacked strong launch games. People who'd bought a Wii to play fitness games didn't see the need to upgrade.

SEQUELITIS

Every time Nintendo has made a revolutionary console that's been a huge hit, they've produced a successor that has sold less well. The SNES sold less than the NES, the Game Boy Advance sold less than the Game Boy, and the 3DS sold less than the DS. But all those consoles did well, just not as well as the originals—whereas the Wii U was Nintendo's lowest-selling console *ever*.

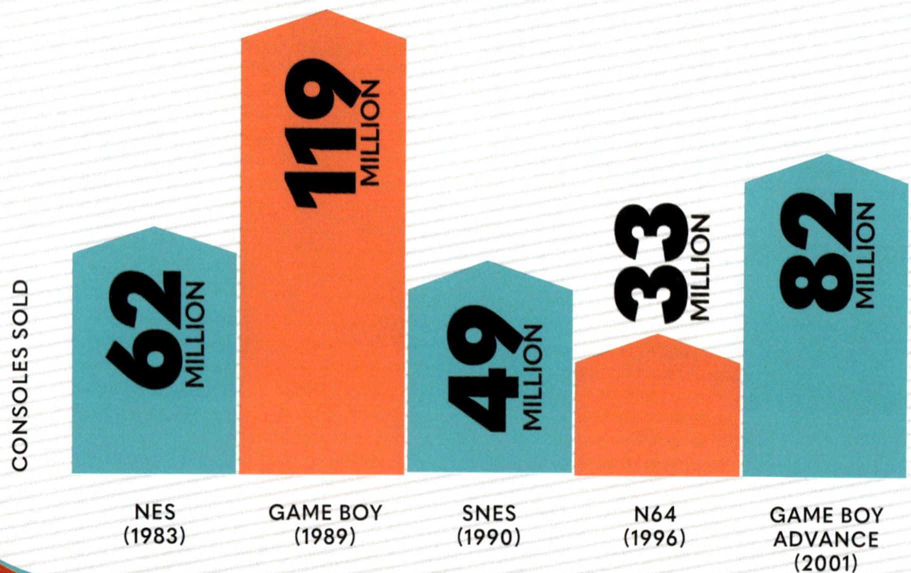

U-TURN

■ Nintendo turned the failure of the Wii U into an advantage for its follow-up console. Design ideas introduced for Wii U were refined for the Switch, and *Breath of the Wild*, which was developed as a Wii U game, became a must-have Switch launch title. Other Wii U games were given ports or sequels on Switch, like *Mario Kart 8 Deluxe* and *Splatoon 2*, and Nintendo made sure other companies were developing for the new console.

Nintendo is in a very different place as they launch the Switch 2, and the world is waiting to see if they can avoid another Wii U situation. As the hardware is so similar to the original Switch, it's relying on new games to catch the imagination of players. But it's clear Nintendo believes hybrids are where it's at!

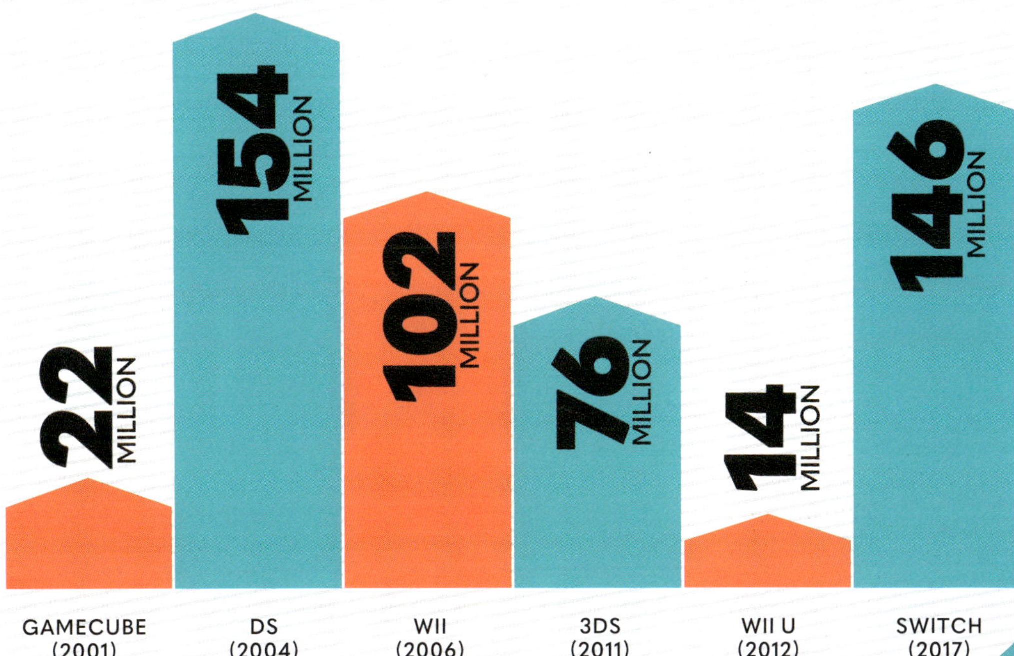

PRINCESS PEACH: SHOWTIME!

THE SHOW MUST GO ON—AND PEACH IS CENTER STAGE!

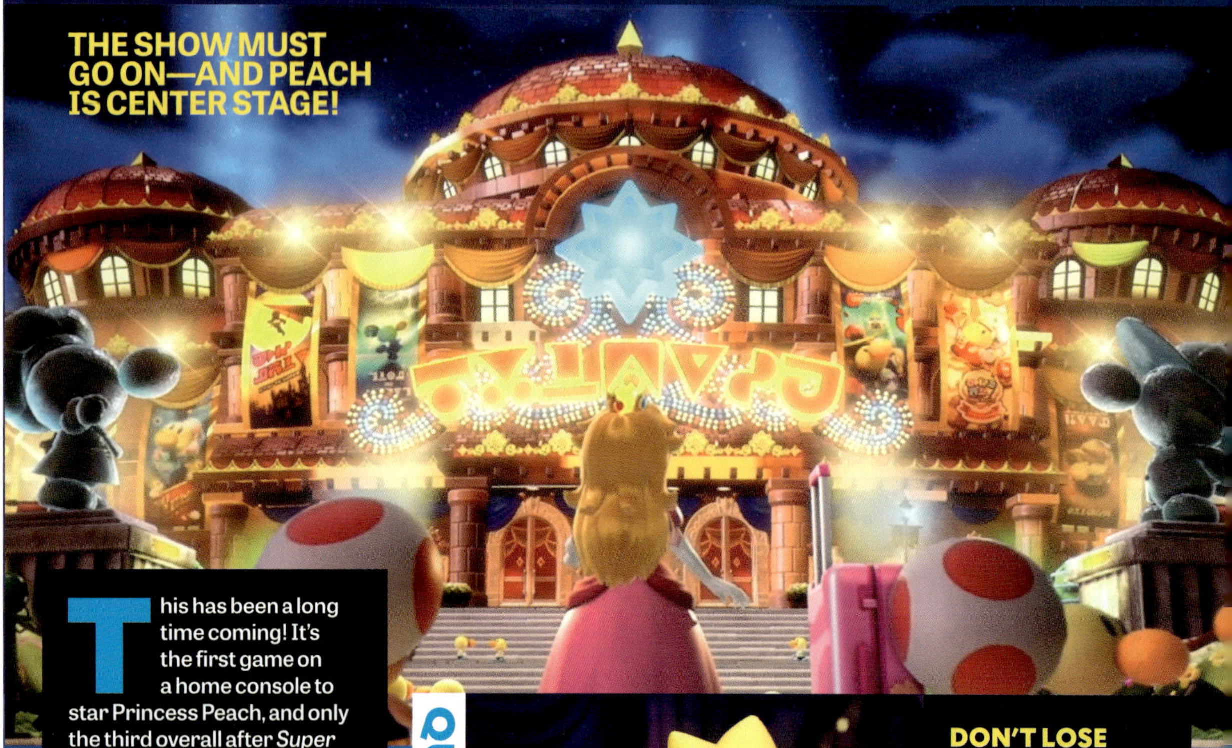

This has been a long time coming! It's the first game on a home console to star Princess Peach, and only the third overall after *Super Princess Peach* on the DS and the watch game *Princess Toadstool's Castle Run* (and we're not even sure we count that one).

In *Showtime!*, Peach gets to be many different Peaches. On a trip to the Sparkle Theater, she sees it taken over by the sorceress Grape and the Sour Bunch. To liberate it and the Sparklas who run it, Peach must go through all the plays, playing different parts. With this and *The Legend of Zelda: Echoes of Wisdom*, Nintendo is finally letting these former serial kidnap victims star in their own adventures!

QUICK TIPS

DON'T LOSE HEART

■ If you're struggling with a level, go to the first floor and talk to the Theets until you get offered a Heart Charm, which gives you three extra hearts.

WEIRD REWARDS

■ Look out for things that seem a little . . . off. Flowerpots without flowers or openings that lead behind the scenery. Inspect them and you may be rewarded!

IN THE SPOTLIGHT

■ Also look out for the faint spots of light that sometimes appear on the ground. These brighten and grow when you get closer. Strike a pose using ZL or ZR.

IN FINE FORM

The Sparkle Theater is a multiplex, with many plays going on across five floors and a basement. Not all of them feel like actual plays, but it's hard to complain when there's this much variety!

STYLE SWITCHING

At a certain point in each play you'll get the chance to transform into one of Peach's other forms—and it feels like you enter a different type of game. Some are action-based, some are puzzle-based, some are something different altogether.

CLOSE COMBAT

So, you can begin playing as Swordfighter Peach, who storms the castle to rescue the king, and Kung Fu Peach, who has a classic martial arts story with a training sequence at the start . . .

BAKE OFF

. . . but then you're Patissiere Peach, who must play minigames based around decorating cakes and baking cookies. Mermaid Peach, meanwhile, has a singing ability you may find familiar if you've seen a certain sea-based Disney movie.

GO FIGURE

With Figure Skater Peach, it turns into a sports game! The difficulty level is set quite low, but replaying each level to get all the gems and other rewards is a challenge—especially if there's just *one* part of it you can't beat.

FAST FACT

Peach has made cameo appearances in the *Zelda* games. In *Link's Awakening*, when Christine sends her picture to Mr. Write, it's actually a picture of Peach; and you can find her portrait in Hyrule Castle in *Ocarina of Time*.

LIKE THIS? TRY THIS:

SUPER MARIO BROS. 3

The third game in the *Mario Bros.* series takes place in a theater-style setting with raising and lowering curtains, as well as different forms for Mario. It seems like a major influence on *Showtime!*

PRINCESS PEACH: SHOWTIME! COSTUMES GUIDE

Take these Peach forms to secret spaces!

You get more than one chance to play as each Peach form—all of them appear twice in the twenty plays on the upper floors of the Sparkle Theater, then once more in the basement. Here are our favorites—along with tips on how to find hidden areas in their Dark levels!

1

Ninja Peach

■ This form first appears on Ninjutsu: The Art of Rapids on level 1. In this, Peach has a Dash ability and a Camouflage ability, activated simply by moving over to a wall. Use this in The Dark Ninja and the Legion of Guards to sneak past the first guard at the maze, and in the next room strike a pose with ZL or ZR to find a hidden area.

2

Cowgirl Peach

■ This one first turns up in Cowgirl in the Wilderness on level 1. You can immediately earn another Sparkle Gem by lassoing and throwing all five barrels before the spotlight hits the boss. In The Dark Locomotive and the Doomed Town, there's a secret area you can access by striking a pose inside the building before the broken train tracks.

FAST FACT

Actress Brie Larson, who plays Captain Marvel, is also a keen gamer and a Nintendo ambassador. "Getting to see Peach play all of these different characters and see how multifaceted she is after all this time is just spectacular," she told *Elle* magazine.

3 Detective Peach

■ Detective Peach first appears on level 2 in The Case of the Missing Mural. She has the ability to deduce things—but be careful, if you apply her Strike of Intuition and you're wrong, you lose a heart! Look out for a green diamond tile in The Dark Museum and the Purple Mystery: Strike a pose on it for a hidden area.

4 Dashing thief Peach

■ This Peach, introduced in The Perfect Infiltration on level 2, has a grappling hook. When you play as her in the basement level The Dark Prison and the Dangerous Trap, there's a hidden area you can reach by striking a pose under the spotlight to the right of the green pole.

Star quality

■ You're guided by Stella, the Sparkle sprite who watches over the theater. Stella oversees the transformations, which means she's more prominent in the first half of the game—once Peach has unlocked a form, she starts the next play for that character already wearing the costume. But Stella can be summoned to refresh your memory of the different abilities.

5 Mighty Peach

■ Ordinary, everyday Princess Peach becomes a sci-fi superhero in Mighty Mission: Alien Invasion on level 3. She's got an Iron Man–style suit that grants super-strength and, later, the power of flight. Look for the triangle on the floor in Dark Space and the Great Meteor, then strike a pose to access a hidden area.

Sky Oceans: Wings for Hire

A new RPG takes flight!

Sky Oceans takes a big chunk of inspiration from *Skies of Arcadia*, an epic RPG that came out on the Sega Dreamcast and saw pirates flying through a world of sky islands. There's also a lot of *Star Wars* in the tale of Glenn Windwalker (yeah, it's not subtle) deciding he wants to become a pilot, fight the oppressive Alliance, and learn what happened to his missing father. And visually it's inspired by Studio Ghibli movies like *Laputa: Castle in the Sky*. It's got lots of good ingredients, but how do they come together?

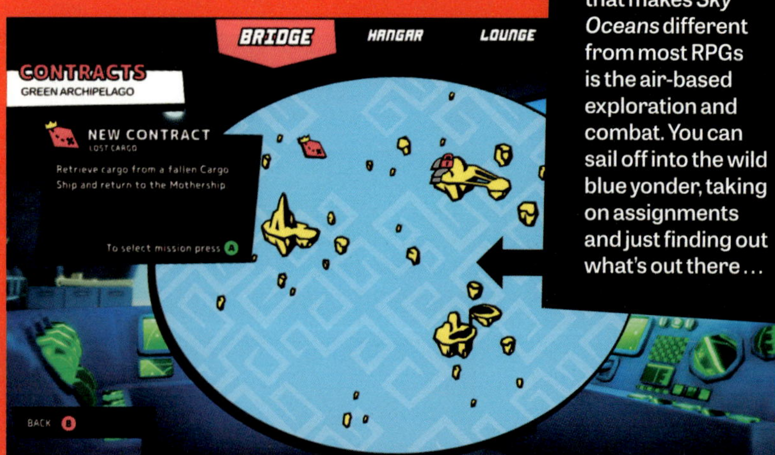

A breath of fresh air

The major thing that makes *Sky Oceans* different from most RPGs is the air-based exploration and combat. You can sail off into the wild blue yonder, taking on assignments and just finding out what's out there…

Winging it

There's a flight-simulator aspect to the game. You travel with three companions and do all the stuff like maintaining speed and altitude. The other party members use their special abilities to help—checking for enemies, clearing paths, and so on.

No return flight

And you can get into dogfights with enemies! This is turn-based combat in the classic RPG style: You assign actions to all party members at the start of a turn. Be warned—if a member of your party retreats, they won't be able to rejoin the fight later!

Make the grade

The bosses get challenging as the game progresses, so keep gaining strength to make sure you're ready for them. When you're not flying, it's vital to buy upgrades for your airship as well as items for your inventory. And, of course, level up your characters with skill points!

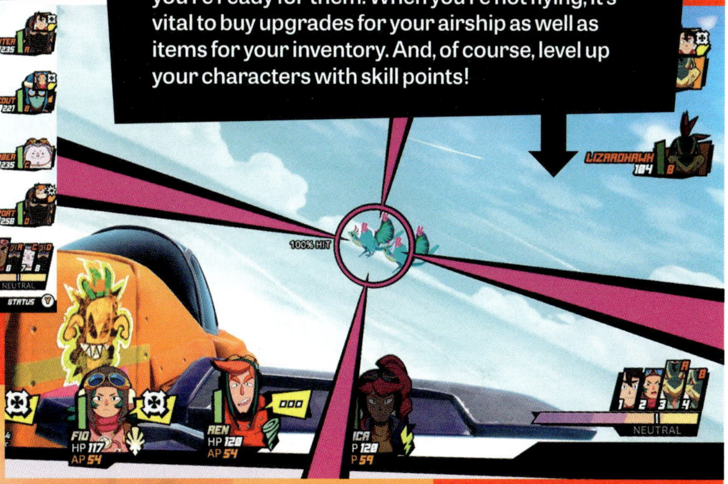

FAST FACT

***Sky Oceans* may look like a classic Japanese RPG, but it was developed by Octeto Studios, which is based in Santiago, Chile. They also made a tactical game called *Cyber Ops: Tactical Hacking Support*.**

An air of mystery

The story is very well put together: It's got an interesting cast of characters and the mysteries keep you hooked, which makes up for the slightly flat, static graphics. There's potential for more stories set in this world!

TOP 10 REMAKES & REMASTERS

The games that were so good, they made them twice!

Video games have a much better sense of their own history than they once did. Old games that might once have been thrown into the dustbin of history, dismissed as too slow or basic, have been reclaimed by retro games lovers—and now they often get a remake or remaster, bringing them to a new generation. Sometimes it's just a case of polishing up the graphics; with others, the entire game is reimagined from the ground up!

10 Yu-Gi-Oh! Early Days Collection

A whole bunch of games based on the ever-popular card game are brought together in this great-value collection, including the *Duel Monsters* games that were only released in Japan and classics like *The Eternal Duelist Soul*. It includes traditional card-battling games and RPGs—enough to keep you going for months, if not years!

AVAILABLE ON: **Nintendo Switch, PC**

09 Star Wars Episode I: Jedi Power Battles

This notoriously tricky platform beat 'em up came out on the original PlayStation and Dreamcast back in 2000, and it's made an all-platforms comeback for its twenty-fifth anniversary. The awkward control system has been overhauled and thirteen characters are unlocked from the start rather than five, but they've kept the successful couch co-op mode.

AVAILABLE ON: **Nintendo Switch, PS5, PS4, Xbox Series S/X, PC**

08 Mario vs. Donkey Kong

■ So many classic Mario titles have been a Switch glow up: *Super Mario 64*, *Super Mario Sunshine*, and *Super Mario Galaxy* are on *Super Mario 3D All-Stars*, then there's *Super Mario RPG*, *Paper Mario: The Thousand-Year Door*—and now *Mario vs. Donkey Kong*, a puzzle-platformer which harks back to the roots of both characters in the original *Donkey Kong*. Originally released for the Game Boy Advance in 2002, it features over 130 levels of Mario trying to get back the Mini-Marios stolen by Kong from Mario Toy Company. Will we also see remasters for the three sequels?

AVAILABLE ON:
Nintendo Switch

07 Dragon Quest III

■ It's less well-known to gamers in the United States, but in Japan the 1988 NES RPG *Dragon Quest III* is revered as a classic: So many kids got into trouble for skipping school to buy it on the day of release, future games in the series were released on weekends instead. Developers Square Enix haven't messed with it too much for this remake: The basic 8-bit graphics of the original have been swapped for a lush storybook style, but the gameplay has a similar feel. There's a new character class of Monster Wrangler, but don't worry—the deliberately awful Gadabout class is still there.

AVAILABLE ON: Nintendo Switch, PS5, Xbox Series S/X, PC

06 Donkey Kong Country Returns HD

■ The *Donkey Kong Country* series isn't just another *Mario* spin-off—the original game is still rated as an all-time great. *Donkey Kong Returns* revived the series for the Wii in 2010 after a long gap, and it divided opinion—some thought it was up to the standard set by the original, but others felt it was overly difficult and frustrating. It's already been remade once for the 3DS, and happily the Switch version includes all the extra levels from that.

AVAILABLE ON:
Nintendo Switch

05 The Legend of Heroes: Trails in the Sky the 1st

■ The *Legend of Heroes* series started out as a spin-off from *Dragon Slayer*, and the sixth game in the series, *Trails in the Sky*, kicked off its own subseries. Like a lot of RPGs, it's big in Japan but has never been that successful elsewhere, and this remake for the Switch aims to change that. The overhauled graphics are remarkable: The overhead view of the original has been replaced by a 3D world with a hand-drawn anime look. One of the best things about this game is the depth of its world: You'll find the NPCs' dialogue changes as the game goes on, creating side narratives you can follow.

AVAILABLE ON: **Nintendo Switch**

04 Apollo Justice: Ace Attorney Trilogy

■ The *Ace Attorney* games were hugely popular on Nintendo's handheld consoles in the 2000s: Mystery visual novels that required the player to listen to evidence, watch out for lies, and successfully defend their clients. The original trilogy was collected as *Phoenix Wright: Ace Attorney Trilogy*, and now the remaining mainline games have been released as *Apollo Justice: Ace Attorney Trilogy*. The four spin-off games—three of which were previously only available in Japan—are also collected on *The Great Ace Attorney Chronicles* and the recent *Ace Attorney Investigations Collection*, so you can play the whole saga!

AVAILABLE ON: **Nintendo Switch, PS4, Xbox One, PC**

03 Braid Anniversary Edition

■ The indie games sector has grown so much since the 2000s, and *Braid* was one of the first to surf that wave when it came out in 2008. Developer Jonathan Blow wanted to do something that stood totally apart from trends in video games: The result was a quirky puzzle game, hailed as a brilliantly original masterpiece with painted-style graphics and a clever time-rewinding mechanism. It still feels like nothing else, and according to Blow, the remaster didn't get much attention and sold disappointingly, so take a look. If you want to make your own games, his commentary may give you some pointers!

AVAILABLE ON: **Nintendo Switch**

02 Final Fantasy VII Rebirth

There are remakes and then there are the *Final Fantasy* remakes. The original *Final Fantasy VII* on PlayStation was a huge game, but the remake is so big it's been split into three. *Final Fantasy VII Remake* came out in 2020, *Rebirth* followed in 2024, and the third is currently in the works. It changes parts of the story to create some surprises for longtime fans, but new players can just enjoy one of the great RPG games in an even more immersive form. You don't even have to have played *Remake* to enjoy *Rebirth*—they're all designed to work as their own thing.

AVAILABLE ON: PS5

01 Luigi's Mansion 2 HD

The release of *Luigi's Mansion 3* in 2019 may have puzzled some players who didn't know there'd been a *Luigi's Mansion 2*. But Nintendo counts the 3DS game *Luigi's Mansion: Dark Moon* as part of the main series, and they've made the numbering nice and neat with this Switch remaster. It's been given the visual style of the third game, but otherwise there are no real changes—and the game doesn't need them, because it's a classic. The multiplayer ScareScraper mode is a particular highlight!

AVAILABLE ON: Nintendo Switch

EPIC MICKEY REBRUSHED

A new coat of paint for a classic.

Considering Mickey Mouse is the mascot of the world's biggest entertainment company, it's surprising how little Disney has done with him in recent decades. Mickey's most interesting outings by far have been in video games, with '90s games like *Castle of Illusion* and *The Magical Quest* bringing back the surreal side to his adventures that had gone missing. *Epic Mickey*, which came out on the Wii in 2010, followed this tradition—and it's been given a spectacular remake for current consoles.

WHAT A WASTE

Mickey has stumbled on Wasteland, a world created by Yen Sid (the sorcerer from the movie *Fantasia*, which is obviously "Disney" backward). Forgotten characters exist here, but now they're under threat from The Blot.

FAST FACT

Warren Spector, director of the original *Epic Mickey*, is best known for the *Deus Ex* games, which combined the RPG and FPS genres and are often listed among the best games of all time.

A WORLD OF WEIRD

It's full of lovely visual touches, such as the moment you have to clamber up a pile of old discarded Mickey merch, and these shine even more in the new HD version. It's a great way to discover a classic game.

GOODY TWO-SHOES

One of the game's most interesting aspects is how Mickey isn't a straightforward good guy. It is his fault Wasteland is in trouble, and the player is given the option to betray characters for their own gain.

BRUSH UP

Mickey's weapon is a magic paintbrush, which he can use to create and erase objects. You can make changes to the game environment to aid your progress—and you can choose to win over your enemies or destroy them.

ACTIONS AND CONSEQUENCES

Watch out if you choose to betray characters—your choices alter the story in the long term. A friend may be able to help you at some later point. It's not quite as dark as it looks, but certainly darker than you might expect a Mickey Mouse game to be.

A BETTER VIEW

Rebrushed makes some welcome tweaks to the original: The erratic camera has been replaced by one you control with the right thumbstick. The side-scrolling 2D mini-levels have also been given new elements to make them livelier.

SHIN-CHAN: SHIRO AND THE COAL TOWN

IT'S MINE, ALL MINE!

The audience for manga and anime in the West tends to prefer action and romance—but in Japan, comedy and slice-of-life series are also hugely popular. *Crayon Shin-chan*, about a mischievous, imaginative, and sometimes rude five-year-old boy called Shin-chan and his family and friends, is a great example. It's in the top ten bestselling manga of all time, ahead of series like *JoJo's Bizarre Adventure*, *Attack on Titan*, and *My Hero Academia* which are far better known in the English-speaking world.

Crayon Shin-chan's humor doesn't always translate well, and while it has spawned dozens of video games, most of them have only been available in Japan. But that's changed recently, with recent games appearing on Switch and PC. Now gamers everywhere can explore Shin-chan's world for themselves!

QUICK TIPS

GO FISH

Rose will block your way to some important areas, and you need to get code words from her three friends. Prince wants you to catch a Masu Salmon, which you can do before going to him.

FIELD A QUESTION

Rose's friend Champ wants a Shiso. Yuno is blocking the field where you get the Shiso, but if you speak to her, she will move two in-game days later.

BEETLE ABOUT

Ace wants you to catch a Rhinoceros Beetle. These are found in the Phantom Fields: Head north and then east—or east and then north—at the Mountain Crossroads.

OUT IN THE COUNTRY

In the manga and anime, Shin-chan usually lives in the Tokyo suburbs, but in *Shiro and the Coal Town*, his dad has to move to a small village for work and the family comes with him.

THE QUIET LIFE

At first, you explore the village as Shin-chan, doing quests to help people as well as wholesome rural activities like bug-catching and fishing (yes, you guessed it—another game with a fishing mechanic).

GOING DOWNTOWN

But then Shin-chan's dog, Shiro, leads him to a mysterious train platform. The train that leaves from here takes him to Coal Town, a mining settlement, where there are also quests for Shin-chan to undertake.

WORLDS APART

The wonky style of Coal Town is quite different from the lush painted backgrounds of Akita, and there are more than a few hints that the whole place is Shin-chan's fantasy.

SLEEP THROUGH IT

Some elements of *Shiro and the Coal Town* are unlocked after a certain number of in-game days have passed—you can make the next day come faster by sleeping. But we suggest using the time to fully explore!

FAST FACT

The *Crayon Shin-chan* anime started in 1992 and is still running today, having notched over 1,200 episodes!

LIKE THIS? TRY THIS:

SHIN-CHAN: ME AND THE PROFESSOR ON SUMMER VACATION

This *Shin-chan* game was made by the creators of the PlayStation series *Boku no Natsuyasumi* (which translates to *My Summer Vacation*), a cult hit in Japan that never got released elsewhere—and it's got a similar vibe.

RACING AHEAD IN SHIN-CHAN: SHIRO AND THE COAL TOWN

Racing trolleys in Coal Town is fun—and rewarding!

Minerals are an important part of *Shiro and the Coal Town*. There are twelve different types in total. They're necessary to complete Invention Challenges, and you can also trade them and use them in sub-missions. There are several ways of getting them, but one is more fun than the others . . .

1 Pick it up

At first, you'll have to get minerals by just finding them lying around. Shiro sometimes helps you with this. Later you'll unlock the Sundries Shop, which sells them: You can buy three of each per day, but the stock will replenish the next day.

2 Win it

A fun and effective way to grab minerals is to do the trolley races, once those are unlocked. The rewards for these include Placer Gold, Shafts, and Tourmaline, as well as rare junk items. You get rewards for winning races but also for hitting high scores, so it's worth revisiting each course until you can break all four points barriers.

3

Race smarter

After the tutorial race, you'll find there are races where the tracks switch, and you may find yourself on an easier path or a higher-scoring one. But on some, like the Herky-Jerky Speed Course, the paths offer the same points—so go for the shorter route. You can see which is which on the map.

4

Keep your balance

There are three trolley types: balance (easy to control but slower), speed (fast but hard to control), and free-cost (comes with an extra free mechanic). Buy the balance trolley Do Your Best 001 as soon as you unlock it: This will see you through Better Pick a Lane, Ultimate Battle Survival, and Thrilling Railway Slalom.

FAST FACT

The creator of *Crayon Shin-chan*, Yoshito Usui, passed away in 2009, but the series was rebooted the following year by members of his studio under the title *New Crayon Shin-chan*.

5

Get the brakes

You'll get the best results by unlocking and purchasing the speed-type trolleys but also the brake upgrades, which give you more control. You can also use strategic speed boosts to get ahead of your opponent in the areas where the gems are between the two tracks, and the racer in the lead is the only one to score! You can use your minerals to craft trolley parts, too.

Bugging out

There are forty-four insects to find and complete the nature compendium. Different insects come out at different times. The majority can be found during the day, and some can also be found in the evening. There are three types of fireflies that only come out at night. The only insect that comes out at all times is the Emma Field Cricket.

EA SPORTS FC 25

IT'S ALL KICKING OFF!

EA Sports FC may not roll off the tongue like *FIFA* did (we think they should change it to just *EAFC*), but it's in no danger of losing its crown as the world's top soccer game. It still holds by far the most licenses, including major ones like the English, Spanish, German, and French leagues, plus the Champions League is here, too, with its strange new format.

However, there are some gaps. Major Italian teams have been prized away by Konami's *eFootball*, and there's no expansion of the women's football licenses. EA's international offering is really poor now, with just one team each from South America, Asia, and Oceania and two from Africa. No Brazil, Nigeria, Japan, or Australia! The way is open for FIFA to license a new official game for the 2026 World Cup…

QUICK TIPS

CHANGE YOUR SHAPE

■ There's more tactical flexibility than in previous games, including on-the-fly options you can switch between on the D-pad. Try setting different formations and tactics for your team with and without the ball.

TAKE IT ON YOUR SHOULDERS

■ Use the shoulder buttons when in possession to tell a teammate to come closer or run into space. You can also use the right shoulder to call for support when defending.

DON'T ALL RUSH AT ONCE!

■ When playing Rush with other human players, make sure one of you stays back to defend—it's easy to all race up the pitch and leave the goalie alone!

EVOLUTION, NOT REVOLUTION

There aren't many major changes to this version of *EA Sports FC*—the main appeal is for fans who want to have the most up-to-date squads. (In fact, we wonder if they'll eventually move to a subscription model instead of putting out a new game each year.)

WHAT A RUSH

There's been a total overhaul of the 5v5 Volta mode, which is now called Rush. It's one of the best modes in the game, and you can play in Ultimate Team, mixing current players and legends, and men and women.

PLAYING SMARTER

If you want to get more in-depth, there are new management options called FC IQ to reflect how real teams work. You can give priorities to specific players, telling them to make more attacking runs or hang back to defend.

THE GAME'S GONE

Graphically it's very slick, with lovely pre-match presentation, but we wish we could say the same about the menus. It was weirdly hard to find things in *EA Sports 24* and it hasn't gotten any better!

TRUE TO FORM

EA keeps getting better at making players and teams feel like their real-life counterparts. A lot of this focuses on the star players, so you'll notice it most when playing with the biggest clubs.

FAST FACT

EA Sports FC 24 **sold slightly less than** ***FIFA 23*****, but made more money through microtransactions on Ultimate Team mode. Ultimate Team is back this year, so be wary of getting sucked into overspending!**

LIKE THIS? TRY THIS:

EFOOTBALL

The free-to-play successor to the legendary *Pro Evolution Soccer* series was mocked for its janky graphics and buggy gameplay when it launched in 2021, but it's improved every year and is worth keeping an eye on.

TOPSPIN 2K25

A FRESH SERVING OF A CLASSIC SPORTS SERIES!

The popularity of tennis games has weirdly fallen off since the 2000s, when *TopSpin* and *Virtua Tennis* were the kings of the genre. In recent years it's dried up so much that fans of the sport have had to make do with 2020's decent *AO Tennis*, using its fan-mod features to add new players and expand its range of courts.

So it's great that the *TopSpin* series has returned for its first new game since *TopSpin 4* in 2011 (though sadly not for Switch owners). As the name *TopSpin 2K25* suggests, it's now being produced by 2K studios, makers of leading basketball, golf, and wrestling games. But is it an ace or a double fault?

QUICK TIPS

GET SCHOOLED

■ The TopSpin Academy, coached by John McEnroe, is a must-play, especially if you're planning to get deep in MyCareer mode—it's a lot of fun and adds depth to your game.

STAY CENTERED

■ Try to keep in the center of the court, and run back there after each shot. Often the player who wins the point will be the one who pulls their opponent out of position.

MIX IT UP

■ Don't be afraid to come to the net. It cuts down your reaction time and you need to be careful not to get lobbed, but playing at the baseline all the time makes you predictable!

CAREER BEST

While *AO Tennis* just had the Australian Open license, *TopSpin* has that and the other three Grand Slams—the US Open, Roland-Garros, and Wimbledon. These form part of a well-designed MyCareer mode.

A SELECT GROUP

The licensed player roster is small. A Grand Slam features over a hundred players in the men's and women's draws, whereas the lineup at launch was just twenty-five—men and women, past and present players.

A SENSE OF HISTORY

It's great to have legends like Serena Williams, John McEnroe, Roger Federer, and Steffi Graf. Not enough sports games let you have fun mixing players from different eras and we'd love to see them go deeper with this.

YOU AGAIN?

The MyCareer mode can feel repetitive, as you keep coming up against the same players over and over again (the pool of male players is especially shallow). Unfortunately, it also makes MyCareer feel less realistic.

TRUE TO LIFE

While the game doesn't offer much quantity, it does offer quality: Each player is well tuned to make them feel like the real-world versions. If they keep making new editions, hopefully they can build that roster up!

FAST FACT

When the last *TopSpin* game came out, Andy Murray (who is playable in this game) hadn't won any of his three Grand Slams or his two Olympic Gold medals.

LIKE THIS? TRY THIS:

EVERYBODY'S TENNIS

Like its stablemate *Everybody's Golf*, this takes an elite sport and makes it accessible and relaxed. Also known as *Hot Shots Tennis*, it came out on the PS2 and deserves a spruce-up for modern consoles!

MADDEN NFL 25

TOUCHING DOWN AGAIN!

Madden used to be the best sports game around, with revolutionary tactical depth. It's still the leading football game, but in recent decades other sports games have outstripped it, and it no longer feels like the prize jewel in EA's sports range.

However, EA has been working to upgrade *Madden* in recent years. They've also revamped the presentation, with decluttered menus and better off-the-field animation in Superstar mode, and for the first time, you can create a female coach for Franchise mode. But what's really important is how it plays—and this edition includes some really smart gameplay tweaks that make it more engaging on the field than it's ever been.

QUICK TIPS

NO QUARTER GIVEN

Don't be tempted to drop back too much with your quarterback—they throw better when they're not dodging around. Let your offensive linemen protect him so he doesn't have to.

RUNAWAY SUCCESS

Learn how to use the new custom stems feature. This allows you to adjust your receiver's run just before the snap, making it longer or shorter.

MEDALING AROUND

Don't skip the Training Camp minigames in Franchise mode. The results of these are locked after you accept them, so keep retrying until you get a medal. These can help upgrade your players!

BOOM TIMES

BOOM Tech is a fascinating new addition to *Madden NFL 25*. This changes player collisions to take into account the strength, weight, and stats of each player, as well as the speed and angle of the collision.

VARIETY SHOW

Longtime *Madden* players will know the tackle animations usually start to feel familiar after a while. BOOM Tech creates more unique animations, but it's not just about the look. The outcome of a collision is also less predictable now.

STICK IT TO 'EM

Madden's Hit Stick—used to apply extra force when tackling—has been in the game for twenty years, but it's been revamped to work with BOOM Tech. It's now more dependent on your angle and timing.

FEEDBACK ON YOUR FAILS

You get feedback on each hit, so it doesn't feel random. You can learn from this and improve! Considering this, it's strange that feedback on kicks and passes, present in previous versions of the game, have been removed.

CARRY IT OFF

It's not just about tackling—carrying the ball also changes with BOOM Tech. There's a Ball Carrier Balance and Recovery system, which you can use to try and absorb those big hits.

FAST FACT

A documentary series, *It's in the Game: Madden NFL*, tells the story of the *Madden* games—it's available to stream on Amazon Prime.

LIKE THIS? TRY THIS:

EA SPORTS COLLEGE FOOTBALL 25

EA's college football series ran alongside *Madden* for twenty years, but came to an end in 2013 due to legal problems. Now it's finally back, and it's more than just *Madden* with different rosters—it feels different and has more depth.

NBA 2K25

BACK FOR ANOTHER SPIN!

The creep of microtransactions has been everywhere in sports games in the last few years, and *NBA 2K25* has often been singled out as the worst offender. Online modes have been impossible to compete in unless you go in for a lengthy grind or pay extra to skip it. And at times it's felt like the actual basketball was an afterthought compared to the re-creation of the lifestyle around the sport.

The latest version makes a few changes to the on-court experience, such as Rhythm Shooting, which takes some getting used to. But mostly it's the same game, and the highlights are a revamped MyCareer mode and the welcome return of the Auction House that gives you a way to acquire cards without buying them.

QUICK TIPS

TIMING IS EVERYTHING

If you're struggling with your shots, try changing the Shot Timing Profile—you may find Normal Risk-Reward more similar to how shot timing worked in previous versions.

GET BOOSTED

If you're trying to build a team for free, be sure to complete all the tutorials and play all the different MyTeam modes. You'll get player boosts from these.

DRILL DOWN

The old stamina system has been replaced by drills at the Gatorade facility—doing these is essential; you can't compete without boosting your players' stamina.

PLAY LIKE A PRO

NBA 2K24 saw the introduction of ProPLAY. This is a system for turning real game footage into animation. In this year's game, it's even better. It's always a thrill to see a player do something just like their real-life counterpart.

MAKING MOVES

This works well with the new Go-To Shots—signature moves used by the real players. These are cool, but it'd be great if the feature was expanded so each player has more than one.

ALONE OR ONLINE?

Microtransactions are an issue in MyCareer, too, but overall in this edition, there's more good single-player action, which means you feel less nudged toward online play where you either pay up or get hosed by people with ninety-plus squads.

WHAT'S THE STORY?

The MyGM mode offers six different backstories you can choose from, but the MyCareer mode is stronger, with a great City hub that's easier to navigate than last year's.

THE GRAVITY OF THE SITUATION

There's also a wild new mode called Gravity Ball, which is kind of *Rocket League* meets *Splatoon*. Unfortunately, this is a paid add-on and only available on next-gen consoles.

FAST FACT

In 2016, tattoo licensing company Solid Oak Sketches tried to claim their artwork had been used in the *NBA 2K* games without their permission, because three players in the game had tattoos they'd copyrighted. Their legal case was dismissed.

LIKE THIS? TRY THIS:

FREESTYLE 2: STREET BASKETBALL

This informal free-to-play basketball game with an anime style has been around for a decade now but still has a strong following and is the best arcade-style basketball game around.

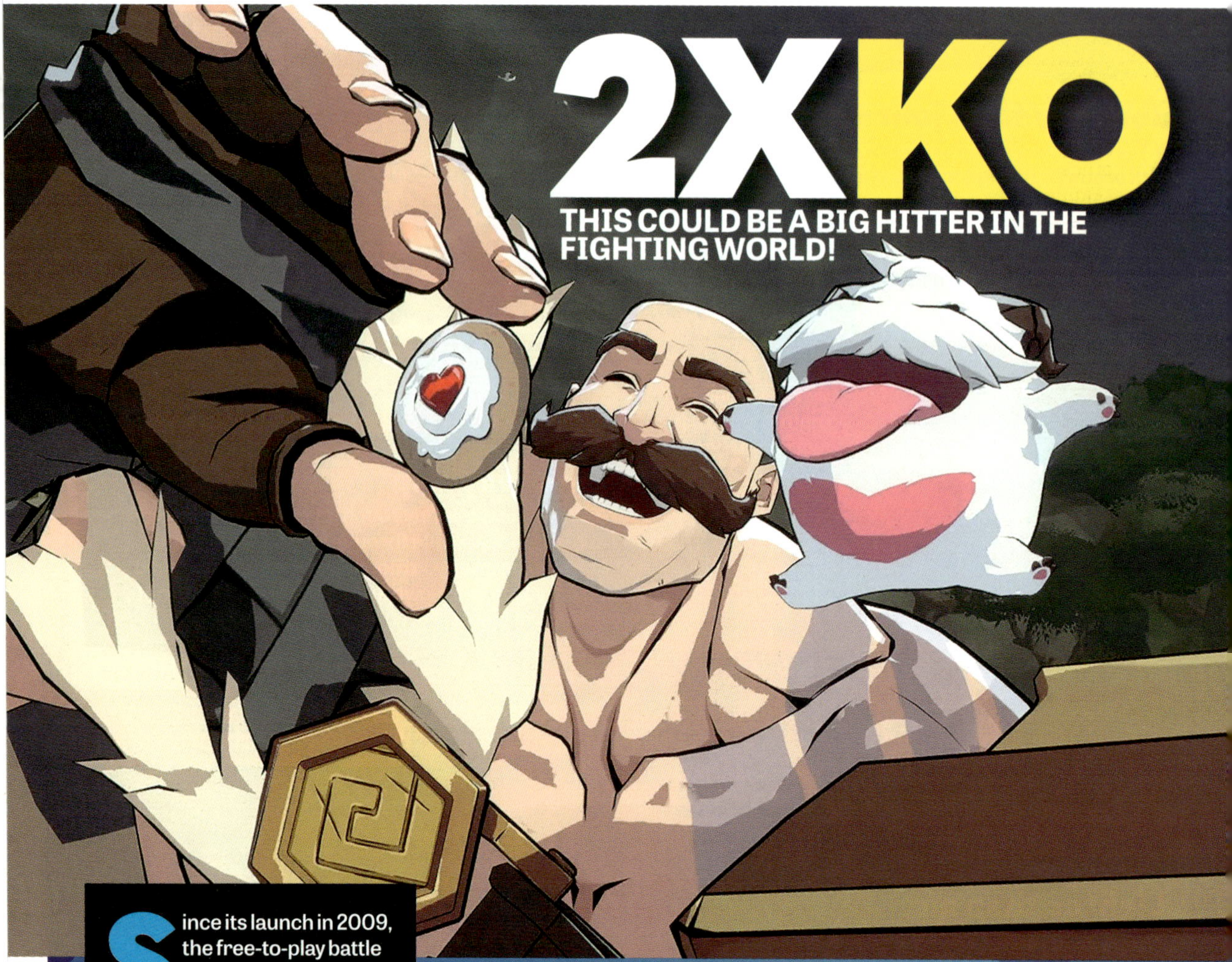

2XKO

THIS COULD BE A BIG HITTER IN THE FIGHTING WORLD!

Since its launch in 2009, the free-to-play battle arena game *League of Legends* has become so popular, its players just call it *League*, which let's face it, would be a really boring title for anything. In recent years the franchise has ventured into other genres via spin-offs like the turn-based RPG *Ruined King* and the sweet, *Zelda*-like adventure *Song of Nunu*.

Now comes another free-to-play title, which allows you to go into combat with the *League* characters in a different way. *2XKO* is a *Street Fighter*–style fighting game that aims to be simple and accessible to newcomers—and offer something different and unique to longtime fighting game fans!

QUICK TIPS

READY TO LAUNCH

All characters have a launcher, which can be executed by pushing down-forward and doing a heavy attack. Perform this at the end of your simple combo.

SUPER SMASH

You can do the light-medium-heavy chain in between other moves to keep a combo going: After launching, try the chain again in the air and then finish with a super.

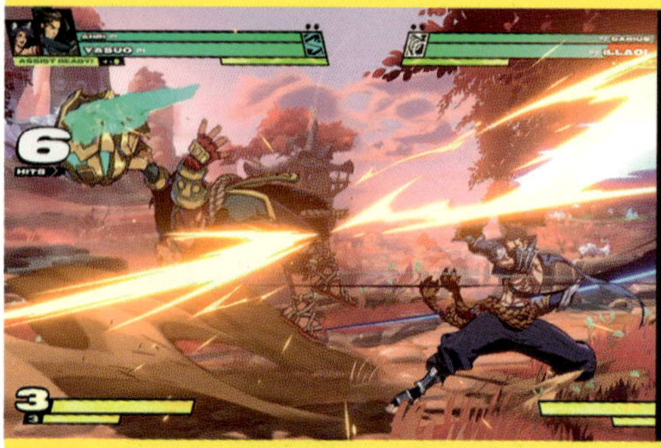

WEIGHT CLASS

If you're not sure how to chain combos, start out by doing light, medium, and heavy attacks in sequence.

SMOOTH MOVES

■ In games like *Tekken* and *Street Fighter*, players have to memorize different elaborate inputs for each character, like quarter-turning the thumbstick before punching, if they want to do special moves. *2XKO* offers a simpler way.

SUPER STRIKES

■ *2XKO* gives you the usual options of light, medium, and heavy attacks, plus two buttons that are used for super moves. The supers drain an energy meter, so you can't just spam them.

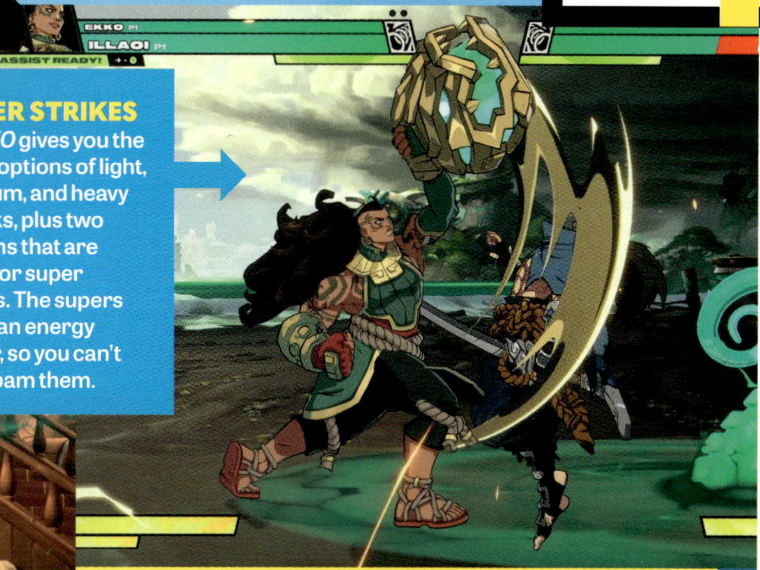

MASH IT UP

■ You can hit buttons to dash and parry, if you want to be more tactical. But you can just mash the main attack buttons and still have fun.

PARRY IT OFF

■ Parrying is different from blocking, which is done in the traditional way by pulling the thumbstick away from the attack. When you parry, you may create an opening to counterattack.

BALANCING ACT

■ Overall, the game does a great job of balancing accessibility with creating enough depth for serious players to develop their own strategies and make themselves really hard to beat!

FAST FACT

***League of Legends* has also spawned an animated series, novels, comics—and music by multiple virtual bands made up of *League* characters. Metal band Pentakill has released three albums, while girl group K/DA has released an EP.**

LIKE THIS? TRY THIS:

UNDER NIGHT IN-BIRTH II SYS:CELES

■ The original *Under Night In-Birth* hit arcades in 2012, and has provided a real challenge to the dominant fighting franchises. The sequel, released early in 2024, retains the original's smart grind meter, which tracks who has the upper hand in each match!

TAKE THE L

2XKO has been a long time coming—it was announced by developer Riot Games way back in October 2019 under the title *Project L*, as part of their tenth anniversary celebrations. At that point it was going to be a one-on-one fighter, but it turned into something different.

GET TO THE POINT

This is a 2v2 fighter with its own style. For each match, you select a team made up of a Point character and an Assist character. You can play with a friend and fight on the same team as an alternative to fighting each other—or four of you can play in teams of two.

SHARE THE LOAD

It's not just about switching fighters when one is low on energy and bringing the other in to finish the fight. You can be really strategic about it! The Assist fighter can take over completely, or they can provide support to the Point fighter.

YOU'RE IT

When you tag the other fighter in, they can continue the combo the first fighter started. This enables you to create combos of even greater variety. You can also do Dynamic Saves, where the Assist fighter stops an opponent's attack.

FUSE THE FORCE

When you start a match, you can select different Fuse options. These allow you to combine your fighters in different ways. For instance, Freestyle lets you tag your comrade in twice in the same combo, while Double Down lets you chain both fighters' super moves together.

FINGER ON THE PULSE

Fury gives you a damage boost when you're on low health. The best for new players is Pulse, which allows you to mash buttons and create combos easily. This is ideal when you're trying to get to grips with a new character, and you can progress to more advanced options later.

DOUBLE KO

In some tag fighting games, such as *Tekken Tag Tournament*, knocking out one fighter wins the match. *2XKO* takes a different approach—you have to knock both fighters out, and a defeated Assist can still help the Point. Last Stand allows knocked-down fighters to make a last-ditch comeback, too!

FAST FACT

Riot Games playtested *2XKO*—and built up some buzz for it—by taking it to *League* tournament events, creating huge lines of eager players everywhere it went!

GAMES BASED ON BOARD GAMES

Video games have been using board games as source material for decades, but the rise of online play means even more demand from tabletop gamers keen to play their favorites with friends when they can't meet up in person. Here are some of the best around...

CATAN

This game of settler colonialism is hugely popular—there's a *Catan* world tournament every two years—and there have been several video game versions of it. In it, you arrive on the island of Catan and must trade, build, and gather resources. While a lot of modern board games take a bit of time to learn, *Catan* is pretty easy to pick up and the tutorial in the latest digital edition, on PlayStation, Xbox, and Switch, makes it even easier.

THE GAME OF LIFE 2

The ever-popular board game where you just do normal *stuff* like going to college, getting a job, getting married, has been around since 1860! The most recent video game adaptation, available on all platforms, has moved things on—it's not just about who makes the most money anymore, and there are thousands of directions you can take your life in. There are also several themes including a superhero world and a moon base.

MYSTERIUM

Most of the classic board games see you playing against one another, but these days there are lots of co-operative board games and *Mysterium* is one of the best. One of you plays the ghost of someone who's been murdered, and the others are mediums trying to solve the murder. The ghost must pass clues to the mediums and hope they work it out. It's great that the digital version offers a way to play it solo, as the board game needs at least four players to work well.

CLUE/CLUEDO

Before *Among Us*, there was *Clue*—or *Cluedo*, as it's called outside North America. There have been many video games based on this classic detective board game, including a 1992 game for the SNES and Genesis, and there's now an edition for Switch, Steam, and phones. To keep it fresh, developers Marmalade Game Studio have added new boards as DLC, so as well as investigating the classic country-house murder, you can go to luxury resorts or a polar research station.

TICKET TO RIDE

The board game is already a modern classic—you're assigned locations at the start of the game and have to build railways that connect them—and the Steam version was spruced up and re-released in 2023. The original map covers the United States and Canada, but we think it's worth getting hold of the Europe and Legendary Asia maps, which give you more interesting landscapes. They have also recently added a San Francisco city expansion set in the 1960s. Groovy!

EXPLODING KITTENS 2

Probably the funniest card game ever made, *Exploding Kittens* has also been a hit because it allows players to be so horrible to one another. For this reason it's best played with people you know, so if you and your friends pick up the Steam version, it's great for online play. The mobile version is also good and cheaper. The best part is the ability to put together your own kitten avatar!

MACHI KORO WITH EVERYONE

The Japanese hit *Machi Koro* definitely feels influenced by city-building video games, so it's appropriate that it's now been given its own video game. You have to build different elements to your city that allow you to construct landmarks: The first player to build all their landmarks wins. *Machi Koro With Everyone* includes digital versions of the original *Machi Koro* and the superior follow-up, *Machi Koro 2*: It brings a lot of extra character to the game, with chibi characters onscreen getting excited by developments.

GLOOMHAVEN

This dungeon crawler has been acclaimed as one of the best board games ever made, and with dungeon crawlers being a popular video game genre anyway, a digital version was inevitable. It's the classic stuff—embark on quests, kill monsters, fight turn-based battles—but it's hard to fault how well done it is here, and it's quicker to set up than the tabletop version!

GET THE NOPE CARDS READY

ROOT

The aim of this strategy wargame is simple: Control a forest. What makes it different from most strategy games is all the factions play slightly differently, with different advantages and disadvantages. The video game version renders the different groups of woodland creatures superbly, and its AI makes it a good solo experience as well as multiplayer. You really need a few plays—using all the different factions—to understand other players' strategies, so there's a lot of depth to it!

WINGSPAN

This very chill strategy game has slightly complicated rules but is awesome when you get the hang of it. The aim is to attract birds to your wildlife reserves, and it's really artful how the actual characteristics of birds have been brought into the game. The design is even more beautiful in the video game adaption—you really feel like you're in the habitat—and the option to play slow online games fits the vibe nicely. It's been enough of a hit that, having already been released on Steam, phones, Switch, and Xbox, in 2024 it was also ported to PlayStation.

The board games-to-video games pipeline runs the other way, too, with many great board games based on video games. Aside from the *Pokémon* card game (obviously), some of the best are *Stardew Valley*, *Slay the Spire*, and *Cuphead*. There's also a great card game based on the enduring educational game *The Oregon Trail*!

Metroid Prime 4: Beyond

Primed for action!

The *Metroid* series has produced some of the most acclaimed games ever made, but it often feels like an outlier at Nintendo: It's got a different vibe from their other franchises, and there have often been loooong gaps between new games. When a game does do well—like 2021's magnificent back-to-basics entry *Metroid Dread*—it almost seems to take Nintendo by surprise.

That hasn't been the case with *Metroid Prime 4: Beyond*, which was one of Nintendo's most anticipated games of 2025, thanks to a combination of delays to its release and new fans coming to the series via Dread and the excellent remaster of the original *Metroid Prime*. Could it live up to expectations?

Lying dormant

Metroid Prime 4 was announced as part of Nintendo Direct way back in 2017, at which point *Metroid Prime 3: Corruption* was already ten years old! The fourth game was originally being developed by Bandai Namco, but Nintendo became dissatisfied with how it was shaping up.

FAST FACT

Metroid **always used to be less popular in Japan than in other countries, but that may be changing—by the end of its first week, *Metroid Dread* had exceeded the lifetime Japanese sales of nearly every previous game in the series!**

Going retro

■ In 2019 development was restarted at Retro Studios, which made the original *Prime* trilogy for GameCube and Wii back in the 2000s. The *Prime* games use a 3D, first-person viewpoint, rather than the classic side view of the original. So ironically it's less retro than *Dread*.

Mighty morphing

■ However, anyone whose first *Metroid* game was *Dread* will recognize the gameplay—exploring confined areas and opening up new pathways using the skills of protagonist Samus Aran. Her Morph Ball form is pleasingly dynamic in 3D, rattling along chutes at pace—and the viewpoint switches here so you can see what you're doing.

An old rivalry

■ The antagonist this time around is Sylux, who was one of the six bounty hunters in the 2006 DS game *Metroid Prime Hunters*. He also previously appeared in the 100-percent completion ending of *Metroid Prime 3*, and the first thing we knew about *Metroid Prime 4* was that it would pick up on this rivalry!

A world of trouble

■ Sylux hates the Galactic Federation, and as Samus operates on their behalf, this makes their rivalry more personal. His raid on a Federation research facility, accompanied by space pirates and seemingly tame Mochtroids, is only the beginning of Samus's problems …

PROMENADE

YOU CAN'T JUST STROLL THROUGH THIS INVENTIVE PLATFORMER!

Classic 2D platform games, in which players make their way through levels by jumping between platforms, were the default video game in the 8-bit and 16-bit eras. And while the gaming world is totally different now, it's still a genre where developers are doing really creative work—such as new French game studio Holy Cap, whose first game, *Promenade*, is full of enthusiasm for the style.

Your aim is to repair the great elevator, which allows travel between worlds. To do this, you need to find the missing cogs. You're aided in this quest by a poulp (that's the name for a creature like a squid or an octopus), who you can fling out to grab things.

QUICK TIPS

FAST FINISHING

■ There are six ultra rare trophies to unlock. The toughest of these is Lightning Fast Promenade!, which you can acquire by completing the game in under two and a half hours.

DEVELOPING SITUATION

■ Beat all the developer times in the time trials and you'll unlock Better Than The Developers! Getting through the Comedian's Lair, and climbing the mountain without falling, also unlock ultra rare trophies.

HOOK, LINE, AND SINKER

■ The ideal moment to dash while drilling is when you're about to reach the surface—you'll get the greatest distance that way.

SAFE-ISH SPACE

The style of *Promenade* is cute and the vibe is cozy: While you can take damage, it regenerates after a few seconds' nap in a hammock. The game is far more about puzzling than battling.

KEEP YOUR ENEMIES CLOSE

At first you may feel frustrated that enemies respawn so quickly after you've destroyed them. But you need those enemies! The key move of the game involves throwing them down to bounce off.

GETTING A BOUNCE

Once you get the hang of it, the game becomes really satisfying to play—and the world gives you puzzles that are nicely intuitive. You'll be required to use some precise movements and timing, too!

BREAKOUT AREAS

Sometimes it's worth tracking back because new abilities create new opportunities. The powerless arcade machines can be fixed, for instance—allowing you to access some classic arcade action!

TAKING NOTES

Soon you acquire a journal you can use to track your achievements. The levels aren't linear: Each area has a set of tasks for you to tick off. The challenges are always changing as you progress through the game.

FAST FACT

Platform games made up just under a third of games on the Sega Master System and a quarter of games on the Mega Drive, but by the 2000s, just 2 percent of games sold were platformers.

LIKE THIS? TRY THIS:

SUPER MARIO BROS. WONDER

While most 2D platformers these days come from the indie world, Nintendo—which created the genre with *Donkey Kong*—brought the *Mario Bros.* series back to its roots with this spectacular effort in 2023.

LIL' GUARDSMAN

TAKE CHARGE OF SECURITY AND GO POWER-MAD!

This charming puzzle adventure is a family-friendly version of the dystopian game *Papers, Please*. Lil is the 12-year-old daughter of a guardsman who lives in the Sprawl, a fantasy kingdom. Dad is a tad irresponsible, and when he leaves his post to indulge in gambling, he leaves Lil to do his job for him. You play as Lil, and it's up to you to decide whether to let visitors in or deny them access.

Thankfully you're not stuck in the guardsman's hut *all* the time: Between shifts you can explore the city and get involved with other storylines. It's like playing your way through a Cartoon Network show!

QUICK TIPS

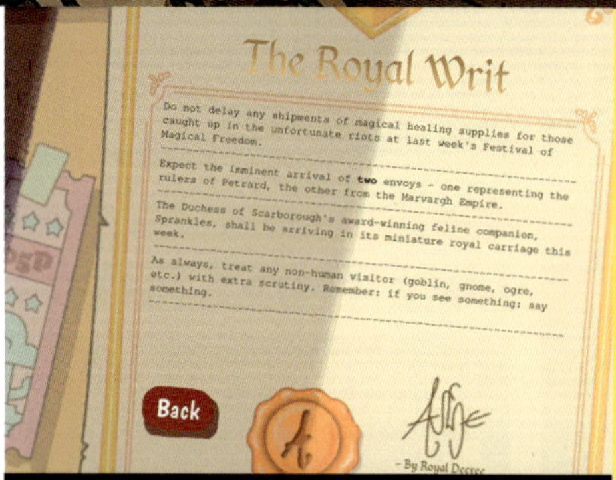

REPLAYS NEEDED

■ There are twenty secret achievements to unlock in the game—not all of them can be completed on a single playthrough, as they involve sending certain characters down different paths.

GAME FOR A BARF

■ Here's a fun one: When you reach chapter 3, interrogate Finius three times and then tease him on every occasion to unlock the Triple Barf! achievement.

TAKE NOTICE

■ Check the noticeboard in the guardsman's hut every day—the announcements that appear there will keep you updated on how your decisions are affecting the world.

ACTION STATIONS

There are three action points you can use on each interaction with a visitor. You can interrogate them, consult one of the royal advisors, or use a tool.

GET A DO-OVER

Helpfully, Lil has also been given an experimental time machine called the Chronometer 3000. This gives you the ability to rewind interactions that go wrong and try again—though there's a limit to how many times.

TOOL UP

Your tools consist of a metal detector, an X-ray machine, a decoder ring, a whip—and an incredibly useful truth spray. Your tools need power crystals to work, though, so you don't have unlimited uses.

STAR QUALITY

You get a star rating each day for how well you've done your job. There's a minimum score you need in order to get paid. If you manage to hit four stars, there are some minor game bonuses to be had.

SUFFER THE CONSEQUENCES

Your actions in this game definitely have a wider impact, so think carefully. You can recruit people to fight in the ongoing war, and your choices can affect who wins that war!

FAST FACT

***Lil' Guardsman* was the first game made by Canada's Hilltop Studios and was nominated for Best Debut at the Indie Game Awards alongside *Arranger*; *Little Kitty, Big City*; *Loddlenaut*; *Mullet Madjack*; and *Worldless*.**

LIKE THIS? TRY THIS:

NO UMBRELLAS ALLOWED

This game set in a dystopian world has a similar focus on one-to-one communications: You work in a secondhand shop and must deal with the people who come in to sell items, haggling for a good price.

CROSSY ROAD CASTLE

The castle that can never be conquered!

Crossy Road, the infuriating but oddly addictive game of traffic-dodging, celebrated its tenth birthday in 2024—and marked the occasion with a wider release for the sequel, *Crossy Road Castle*. This was exclusive to Apple Arcade when it came out in 2020, but is now available on PS5, Switch, and Xbox Series S/X. In this game you don't crossy road, you climby castle. Should they have called it *Climby Castle* instead? Discuss.

DOOR TO DOOR

Crossy Road Castle is made up of a huge number of mini-levels. You enter through one door and exit through another, and then the castle twists around to reveal the next level on the next side. However…

ROOM ROULETTE

The smart thing is this: After the first level, they appear in a random order! Every playthrough is different. It's classic platforming—you have to move and jump, avoiding obstacles and enemies, and you have three lives.

CROSSY CO-OP

There's a great multiplayer co-op mode—only one player needs to reach the door to complete the stage, and if any of you died on the way, you get those hearts back! It's an awesome party game.

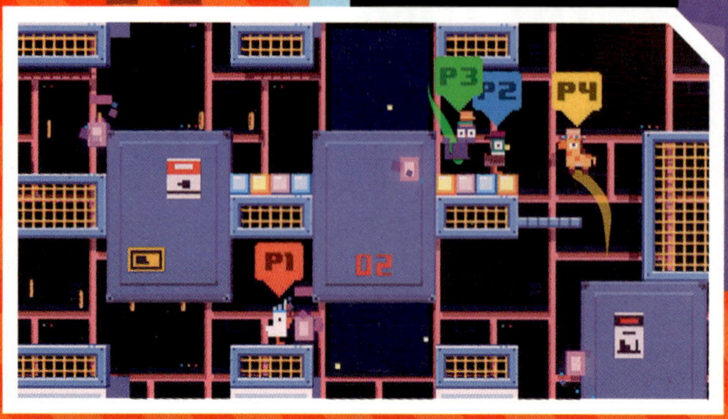

VEND FOR YOURSELF

Every ten levels there's a vending machine to top up your lives, and every thirty levels there's a boss. Each boss you defeat earns you at least one purple coin, and there are other such coins to be found.

CHARACTER BUILDING

Fifty coins are needed to operate the character dispenser, because it wouldn't be *Crossy Road* if you couldn't unlock more characters. You'll need to get grinding if you want them all—but it's an addictive game, so that's not a problem!

FAST FACT

Crossy Road was partly inspired by *Frogger*, an arcade hit from 1981 in which the player must guide frogs across a busy road without getting splatted by cars. *Frogger* also has floating log sections!

BEEN HERE BEFORE?

Thanks to the procedurally generated levels, there are apparently around 80,000 possible mini-levels in *Crossy Road Castle*. Not bad replay value—you could play every day for months and never see them all!

Marvel Rivals

Watch out, *Overwatch*—here come Earth's mightiest heroes!

At the end of 2024, Marvel entered the free-to-play world with its own battle game. Rather than using the battle royale approach (there's plenty of Marvel in *Fortnite* anyway), *Marvel Rivals* uses *Overwatch*-style gameplay, with players divided into two teams of six.

Rivals launched with five different game modes. In Conquest, both teams seek to pick up the points dropped when a hero is eliminated. In Convoy, one team must escort a moving object through the map, and in Convergence, one team tries to capture a series of checkpoints. In Domination (they ran out of names beginning with "con"), both teams must attack and hold a point on the map, while Doom Match is a free-for-all fight to the death!

Class acts

There are three classes of fighter—Vanguard, Strategist, and Duelist. Broadly, these are like the Tank, Healer, and Damage Dealer classes seen in other types of games. But even within these classes, different heroes play very differently.

Shark life

It's great fun trying out all the classes and seeing which one suits your play style best. There are so many classic characters on the roster, like Iron Man, Hulk, and Jeff the Land Shark. (What do you mean you've never heard of Jeff the Land Shark?)

Group dynamics

Certain heroes can team up in groups of two or three to produce new effects—this is called Dynamic Hero Synergy. And some characters have more than one synergy group. Spider-Man can team with fellow Spider-People Peni Parker or Venom, but also with Squirrel Girl.

Besties

Some synergy bonds are obvious—you won't be surprised to find Rocket works well with Groot (and Jeff the Land Shark). Likewise, Hawkeye and Black Widow have synergy, and Mister Fantastic and the Invisible Woman are a particularly strong pairing.

FAST FACT

Jeff the Land Shark—a shark who lives on land—was created for the comic book *West Coast Avengers* in 2018, the pet of Gwenpool and Hawkeye (the Kate Bishop version). He was popular enough to be given his own digital comic in 2021.

Hitting it off

Some combinations are more surprising. When Iron Fist and Luna Snow work together, his damage increases, and she projects an ice ring that damages enemies and heals allies. Scarlet Witch, meanwhile, can imbue Magneto's sword with chaos magic!

TOP 10 NEW INDIE GAMES

Looking for some quirkier gaming? Here you go!

Some of the best indie games of the past year have put new spins on familiar genres, but others have given us really creative and original experiences. Here's our top ten (not including games about cats, which we gave their own section because there are so many).

10 Parcel Corps

Like the 1980s classic *Paperboy* updated for the modern world—with a bit of *Crazy Taxi* and *Tony Hawk* thrown in for fun—*Parcel Corps* sees you playing as a courier making deliveries on your BMX. In between those, you can take on extra quests like time trials, trick challenges, and drone destruction. It's a little repetitive, but mastering the bike is a lot of fun!

AVAILABLE ON:
PS5, Xbox Series S/X, Xbox One, PC, Linux

09 Tiny Glade

This is so cozy and relaxed we're not even sure it counts as a game, but it's a great way to spend time. It's a building game where you make charming little villages, much closer to *Minecraft* in creative mode than *Sim City*. There aren't really any challenges or objectives: You just build, and then you admire it. It could do with a little more depth, but maybe updates will fix that.

AVAILABLE ON:
PC, Linux, GeForce Now

08 Core Keeper

Maybe you think the world doesn't need another sandbox survival game when it has *Minecraft*. But just as *Terraria* created a cool variant by making it a 2D side scroller, *Core Keeper* goes for an overhead view like *Stardew Valley*. It's got more of an RPG element than other sandbox games—you can focus on gathering resources to explore its world more fully and heading out to battle the creatures that live there—but you can also play it as a purely creative game.

AVAILABLE ON:
Nintendo Switch, PS5, PS4, Xbox Series S/X, Xbox One

07 Reka

This pleasingly weird adventure sees you playing as a witch in 19th-century Europe. You travel around with your house, which has Baba Yaga–style chicken legs. This is ingenious because it lets you do all the home-customization stuff from *Stardew Valley*, *Animal Crossing*, and about eight million games on *Roblox*, but you also get to enjoy your house even when you're off adventuring. You travel around and help the villagers out. If you enjoy doing the lower-stakes quests from *Tears of the Kingdom*, this could be the game for you!

AVAILABLE ON:
PC

06 One BTN Bosses

Many indie games make an art of simplicity, and *One BTN Bosses* is a great example. You tackle a series of hectic boss fights, as your ship circles the enemy on a fixed track. You have one button you can use, which reverses your direction so you can avoid their return fire—or at least, that's how it starts off. You can unlock different functions for the button, but you still have just one button to fight with. It can be frustrating, but it's also really addictive!

AVAILABLE ON:
PC

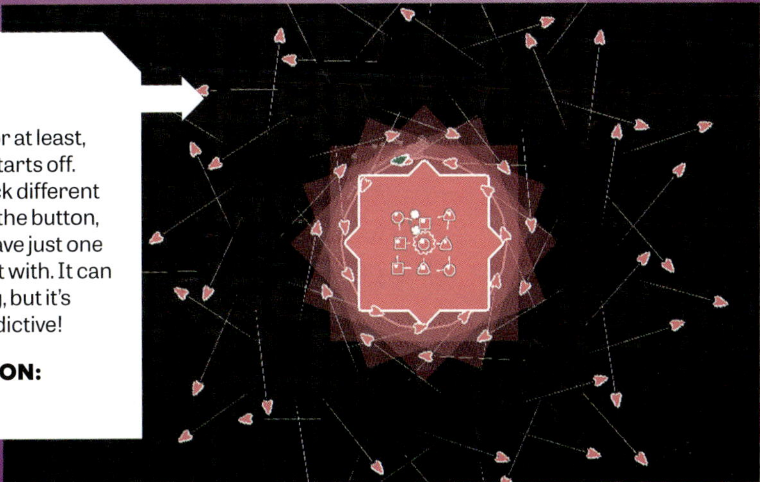

05 The Stanley Parable: Ultra Deluxe

■ *The Stanley Parable* was one of the standout indie games of the 2010s, a funny and surreal adventure game where you play as a man called Stanley wandering around the office where he works. It's not only been given a remaster for its *Ultra Deluxe* re-release, but a whole game's worth of extra material has been added. It's hard to talk about without spoiling the experience for anyone who's never played it before—just give it a spin!

AVAILABLE ON:
Nintendo Switch, PS5, PS4, Xbox Series S/X, Xbox One

04 Another Crab's Treasure

■ Some indie games have a premise that's so creative, and has so much instantly obvious potential, you can't help but smile. In *Another Crab's Treasure* you play as Kril the hermit crab, whose shell has been taken away. He must use pieces of ocean trash as temporary shells as he sets out to get it back. It's a *Dark Souls* type game (or soulslike) without the darkness or the punishing difficulty level, but it still poses a challenge!

AVAILABLE ON:
Nintendo Switch, PS5, Xbox Series S/X, Xbox One, Xbox Cloud Gaming, PC

03 Tactical Breach Wizards

■ This turn-based tactics game has been a huge hit on Steam. You take charge of a team of up to five outcast wizards, each with different skills, and set out to take on private militias. Its urban fantasy setting makes it an enjoyable cross between trad RPGs and military special ops games, and while it's not the most challenging game you'll ever play, the characters and dialogue are excellent, influenced by the great comic writer Douglas Adams. From the pre-combat banter and post-combat anxiety dreams, this is pure joy.

AVAILABLE ON: PC

02 The Plucky Squire

■ This platformer has a pleasingly meta premise: The evil Humgrump has worked out he's the bad guy in a storybook and therefore destined always to be defeated by his nemesis, the heroic Jot. He kicks Jot and his pals out of the book, leaving them to fend for themselves in the real world while he wreaks havoc in the storybook world. The result is really clever, with Jot hopping between 2D and 3D, and lots of great ideas and game mechanics have been thrown into the mix.

AVAILABLE ON:
Nintendo Switch, PS5, Xbox Series S/X, PC, GeForce Now

01 Lorelei and the Laser Eyes

■ *Lorelei and the Laser Eyes* was made by the same Swedish developer as the spectacular runner game *Sayonara Wild Hearts*, and is also nothing like it. It's a survival horror puzzle game, it's incredibly clever and very spooky—and it's narrated by rapper Queen Latifah. There's no opening cutscene filling you in on the backstory—you take control of Lorelei as she stands in the woods and make your way to the monochrome Hotel Letztes Jahr, where you seem to be part of an art project. It's complex, but rewarding, and the story is great!

AVAILABLE ON:
Nintendo Switch, PS5, PS4, PC

FAST FACT

The creators of *Lorelei and the Laser Eyes* suggest you keep a pen and notepad next to you as you play. "We're big fans of pen and paper ourselves, especially for working," designer Simon Flesser told *Nintendo Life*. "My best ideas come when I am writing and sketching notes, usually on a train."

MAXING OUT SONIC X SHADOW GENERATIONS

Tips to help you tackle one of Sonic's best adventures!

The original *Sonic Generations* came out in the era of the PS3 and Xbox 360, and as the name suggests, it brought together the classic 2D *Sonic* and the modern 3D *Sonic*. With revamped versions of stages from across the series, it was hailed as the best Sonic game in years—and now it's back with added Shadow.

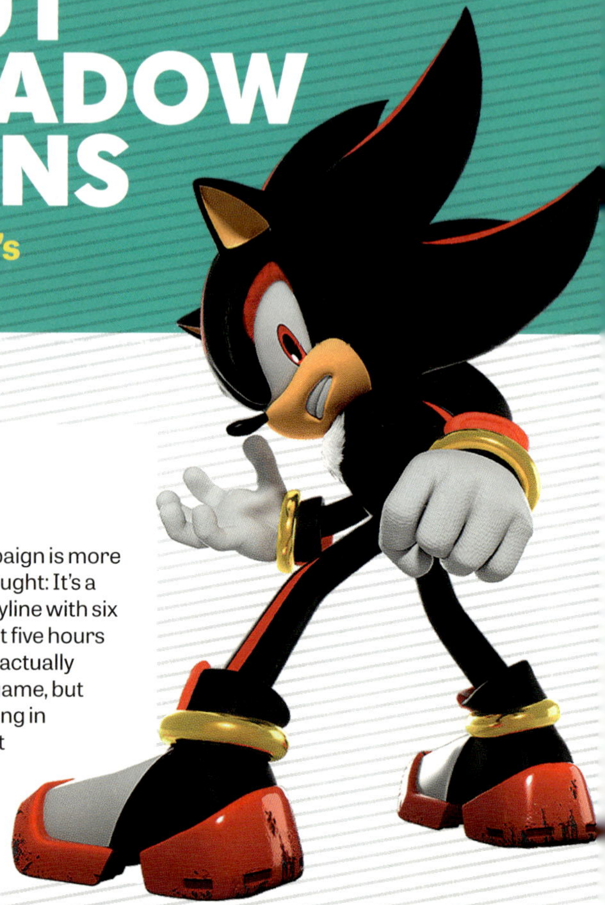

1

Out of the shadows

■ The Shadow campaign is more than just an afterthought: It's a whole separate storyline with six new zones and about five hours of gameplay in it. It's actually the best part of the game, but we suggest not leaping in and playing it first—it makes more sense after you've played Sonic's storyline!

2

Finding the angle

■ Some players have had issues with the camera on 3D *Sonic* games, finding it doesn't give them enough reaction time for the game's speed. So it's worth noting you can alter the camera settings in *Generations* to make it work for you.

FAST FACT

The original *Sonic Generations* has a hidden version of the first *Sonic* game—a Mega Drive controller can be bought at the Skill Shop, which enables you to play a Mega Drive located above the Green Hill portal!

3

Doom-monger

When you replay Sonic's stages after unlocking new abilities, you can discover new pathways. The same is true of Shadow, who unlocks Doom Wing after completing his story. You can use the wings to fly and take shortcuts—if you had these the first time around, they'd make the game much too easy!

4

Do it in stages

In both versions of the campaign, it's better not to get too hung up on collecting everything: Leave it for a replay. Screenshot anything you can't access and come back to it. Also bear in mind Shadow continues to have access to all his abilities for the 2D stages, whereas Sonic is limited to his classic moves.

Shadow play

Shadow was created for the 2005 Dreamcast game *Sonic Adventure 2*. That was planned as his only appearance, but he was so popular he was brought back for *Sonic Heroes* and a controversial "dark" spin-off game, *Shadow the Hedgehog*, in which he used guns. We think *Generations* is easily his best appearance, though!

5

Fresh sounds

Whichever character you play as, make sure you explore the hub world: There are plenty of collectibles there, including new music tracks. The *Sonic* games are known for their great music, and this game continues that tradition—you can also choose to hear these tracks in any level, which makes a nice change if you're replaying levels!

Flock

Flocked and reported!

■ This gentle and colorful exploration game plays like a more relaxed take on Pokémon. You fly through its landscapes on the back of a bird, looking for the whistles stolen from your zoologist aunt Jane by creatures known as Burgling Bewls. While you send sheep to graze the meadows and uncover the missing whistles, you can discover other creatures.

It's all about getting in tune with the world, working out what times of day you need to search and knowing where to look: You'll learn what environments different creatures live in and where they like to hide.

Smooth ride

■ When a game is so heavily based around enjoying being in the environment, it's important that being in the environment is enjoyable, rather than frustrating. The movement in *Flock* is beautifully smooth, and you feel in complete control.

What's that?

The design of the world is also really important. Offering things for the player to find is only part of it—you also want to give them an entertaining experience while they do it, and the odd, goofy designs of *Flock* certainly offer this.

Flocking together

When you find an animal, you don't so much capture them as win them over: You play a minigame, and then they become part of the flock of animals that follow you around. This simple idea adds to the sense of progress.

Be still

Like real nature spotting, you need to use different senses: Some creatures will make a distinctive sound. As well as gliding around to explore and examine different areas, you can find a perch and examine an area in detail.

FAST FACT

One of the designers of *Flock* was artist Richard Hogg, who also worked on *Hohokum*, an indie game where you explore levels by controlling a snakelike kite thing.

Have patience

To get the most out of *Flock*, you need to embrace its change of pace. So many games are fast and furious, and this is the opposite: It makes you wait. You can also share the experience with friends by playing online.

POCKET BRAVERY

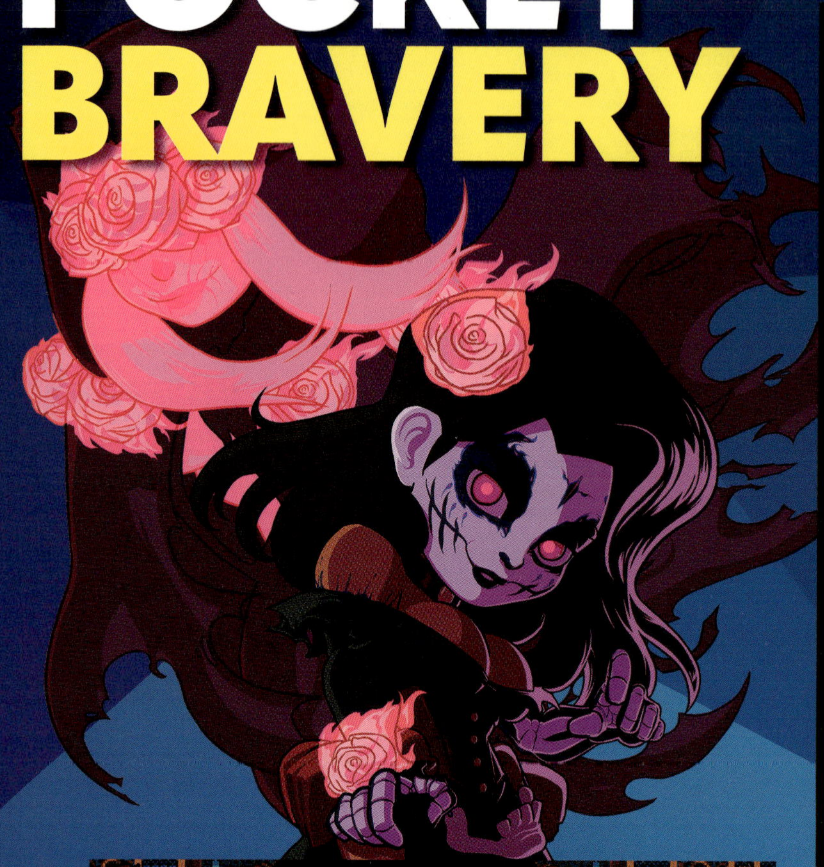

SOCK 'EM RIGHT IN THE POCKET!

In 1997, Capcom released a *Street Fighter* arcade game called *Pocket Fighter*. (Well, it was called that in Japan: In the rest of the world it was *Super Gem Fighter Mini Mix*. Snappy!) This featured characters from *Street Fighter* and other games in "super deformed" versions—that's the manga style where the characters are made stocky and cute.

Fast-forward to the 2020s. A new Brazilian developer called Statera Studio wanted to make a fighting game called *Bravery* but knew a detailed fighting game was too ambitious for a small company. So they used a simpler 2D pixel-art style and created the "pocket" version of a game that didn't exist yet, calling it *Pocket Bravery*. Confused? There's no need to be—this is straightforward classic fighting action.

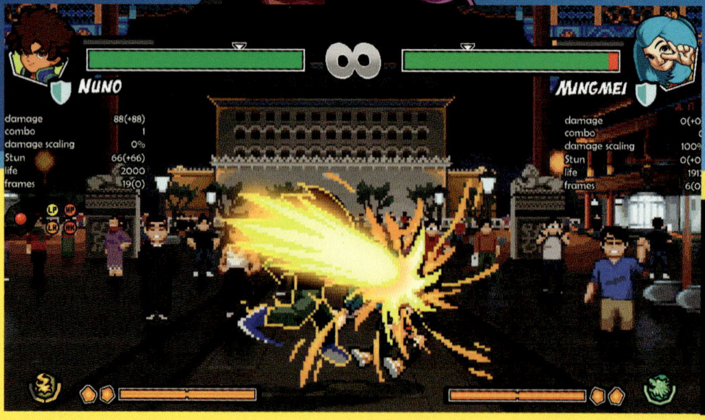

QUICK TIPS

POWER BLOCK

The power bar that fills as you fight isn't only for special attacks—it can also be used to block your opponent's special attacks!

LOW BLOWS

Blocking while standing still allows your opponent to use low attacks. A crouching block will protect against these but leaves you open to air attacks!

FALLING WITH STYLE

The double-punch button also allows you to evade attacks—and if you're falling, press it just as you reach the ground to land safely.

WHAT'S GOING ON

Pocket Bravery has a story mode, with a narrative involving people around the world acquiring strange powers and a terrorist group stealing precious relics. But you can ignore that and go for straight arcade action if you prefer!

ON A BREAK

Pocket Bravery takes influence from lots of different 1990s fighting games, and it even takes a character from one of them—Sho Kamui originally appeared in the Neo Geo game *Breakers*.

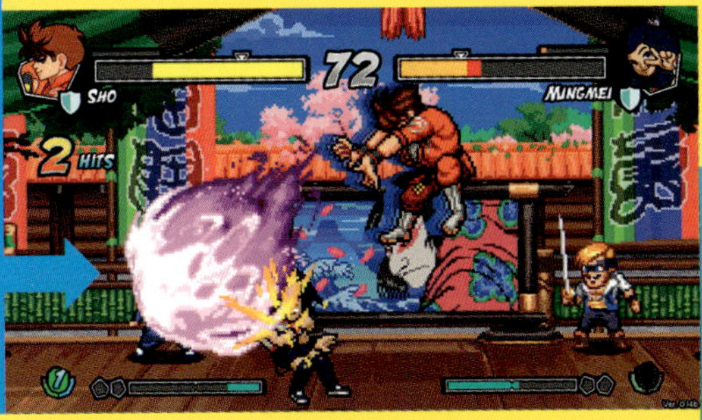

AT THE DOUBLE

You can combine buttons to create moves. The right shoulder buttons unleash double punches and kicks, while the left shoulder buttons are for throws and "breakers" that block attacks and break combos.

DUAL STRENGTH

Whereas the 1990s *Street Fighter* games used three buttons each for punching and kicking, with light, medium, and heavy strikes, *Pocket Bravery* uses a system more like *Street Fighter*'s rival, *Fatal Fury 2*, with just two strengths of punch and kick.

GOING BASIC

And there are the usual button-combo special moves. If you find that too confusing, or you struggle with physical coordination for whatever reason, there's an option to switch to simpler controls!

FAST FACT

***Pocket Bravery* won Brazilian Game of the Year at the Brazil Game Awards and the Flow Games Awards!**

LIKE THIS? TRY THIS:

STREET FIGHTER 30TH ANNIVERSARY COLLECTION

Of the classic 2D *Street Fighter* games, we rate *Street Fighter II Turbo* as the best—but this compilation includes all the main series games from 1987's *Street Fighter* to 1999's *Street Fighter III: 3rd Strike* so you can try them for yourself!

BUST SOME MOVES IN POCKET BRAVERY

Getting started with those specials!

As in any classic arcade fighting game, each character in *Pocket Bravery* has a range of moves that require you to combine patterns on the thumbstick with button presses. The training mode is great for working these out and learning to perform them reliably. Here are some to start you off!

1 Nuno

Nuno has several moves that can be executed by pushing down and then toward or away from the opponent, then either punching or kicking. Explosion Fist and Contempt can be done this way. He also has Elemental moves that involve pushing toward the opponent and then hitting both punch buttons or both kick buttons.

2 Mingmei

Mingmei's Ying/Yang ranged move is activated by pushing toward your opponent before pushing down , then diagonally down-toward before hitting punch. If you use a light punch, you can then add a heavy punch for a second attack. Hit down, then toward the opponent and punch or kick for more moves.

FAST FACT

The original *Pocket Fighter/Super Gem Fighter Mini Mix* is available as part of a compilation of ten games called *Capcom Fighting Collection*, released on all major platforms in 2022.

3

Arshavin

■ Most of Arshavin's moves are done with a quarter-turn of the thumbstick, starting from down and either turning the thumbstick toward your opponent or away from them. If you do either of these and hit kick, you'll do the Bear Charge (away) or Russian Express (toward).

4

Sho

■ As with Arshavin, you can perform several of Sho's moves by quarter-turning the thumbstick. You can also do moves with multiple strikes—his Kurenai Sandan Geri requires a quarter-turn away from the opponent followed by three kicks of either strength. Push toward your opponent, then away, then toward again followed by punch for Shippu Seiken Tsuki.

5

Ndidi

■ Pushing down then up, or away from the opponent and toward them, is the key to many of Ndidi's moves. The vertical version of his Shoulder move uses down-up and then punch, and is effective against aerial attacks. On the ground, try down twice before punch to execute Fall.

Joining the party

■ Pocket Bravery's base roster consists of thirteen playable characters, some of which have to be unlocked. More are being added during each season of gameplay—if you buy a season pass! Characters added in the first season include another guest—Rick Johnson from the action platform game *Guns N' Runs.*

GUNDAM BREAKER 4

IF IT AIN'T BROKE, DON'T FIX IT!

Gundam is another of those big Japanese properties that's spawned a wild number of video games—about 250 in total! The *Gundam Breaker* series of hack-and-slash games started out on PS3, and after three Japan-only releases, it went global in 2018 with *New Gundam Breaker*. Unfortunately, this went down poorly with the series' fan base.

When a series goes back to its old numbering, it's often a clue something's gone wrong and they're trying to fix it, and so it is with *Gundam Breaker 4*. This is a return to form, with addictive gameplay and customization options that give you all the fun of building the model robot kits—without the messy glue!

QUICK TIPS

FINE-TUNE IT

■ Make sure you check the options for adjusting your controls—you may find a setup that suits you better!

GO FOR GOLD

■ Look out for the gold spots on your radar—these optional enemies can be hard to find, as they may be hidden tanks or mini Gundams, but they offer *big* GP rewards.

YOUR BIG BREAK

■ You'll encounter gold enemies more often when using a Breaker Booster—which also increases part drops. You earn a Breaker Booster for each S rank and can turn them on before missions.

A GAME ABOUT PLAYING A GAME

The story of *Gundam Breaker 4* is quite meta: Your character is playing the game *Gundam Breaker 4*, forming a crew of "online players" who are actually NPCs. If you see what we mean.

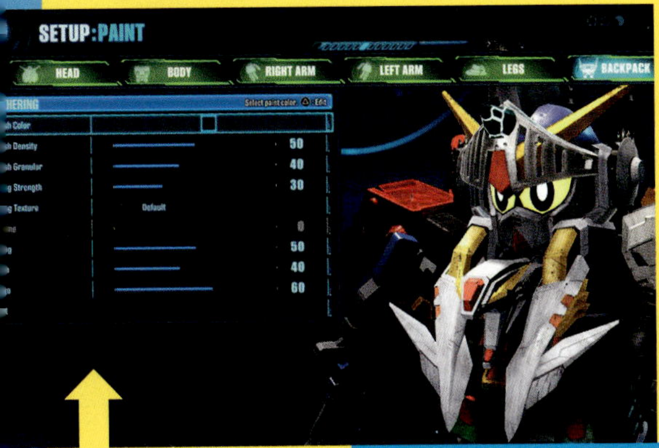

CUT TO THE CHASE

The game-within-a-game thing means the story isn't the most engaging you'll ever play—it's just an excuse to build a Gundam and send it out on combat missions really.

A WORLD OF CHOICE

This is where customization comes in. There are so many parts, paint styles, and avatars, you'll want to unlock more and more. And then you get into the options for using those parts, resizing them to make original designs... There's so much to discover.

BETTER AND BETTER

It can be slow to get started as you need to take on some missions and unlock optional battles. But once you're in, you start getting rewards—and you just want to keep playing!

PICTURE PERFECT

Naturally this comes into its own with *actual* online play, as you can show off the components you've unlocked and how cool your designs are! You can also design your own dioramas, showing off your robots in action.

FAST FACT

***Gundam* started in 1979 with the anime *Mobile Suit Gundam*. It was canceled after less than a year due to low viewing figures, but the popularity of models based on the series made it a mega-franchise!**

LIKE THIS? TRY THIS:

GUNDAM EXTREME VS. MAXIBOOST ON

This PS4 title is a tag-team fighter, which demands a surprisingly tactical approach. It's got a huge roster for a game of this type—more than 180 fighters!

GUNDAM BREAKER 4: GETTING IT TO WORK FOR YOU

It's a game of many parts!

In terms of customization options, *Gundam Breaker 4* is great, but there are so many choices to make, it's easy to get confused. Here's a beginner's guide to earning parts faster and what to do with them when you get them!

1 Work for it

What makes progression in *Gundam Breaker 4* really satisfying is you need to earn parts by breaking them off your opponents (hence the name of the game). And there are ways to increase the chance of part drops, which you can use to farm the parts you most want!

2 A combo of combos

There are two combo meters to watch—one that tracks your kills, and one which goes up when you land a hit. These meters add buffs that can give things like shorter cooldowns—or higher drop rates! Keep your streak going to get the benefit of those buffs!

Stick to your guns

3

■ You have four weapon slots—two long-range, two close-range. At first you can only improve your weaponry by swapping it out for better gear, but at Chapter 3, you unlock the ability to upgrade each weapon—which is great if you want to stick with a favorite. You can also add abilities to your weapons.

4

Skill issue

■ You can make a lot of changes to your play style by checking out the skills that come with each part. You can equip up to four Extreme Skills and eight Option Skills, so the possible combinations are huge! In particular, check what EX Skills each part offers when you acquire it.

FAST FACT

The Gundam model kits, known as Gunpla, make up an incredible 90 percent of all plastic model kits sold in Japan!

5

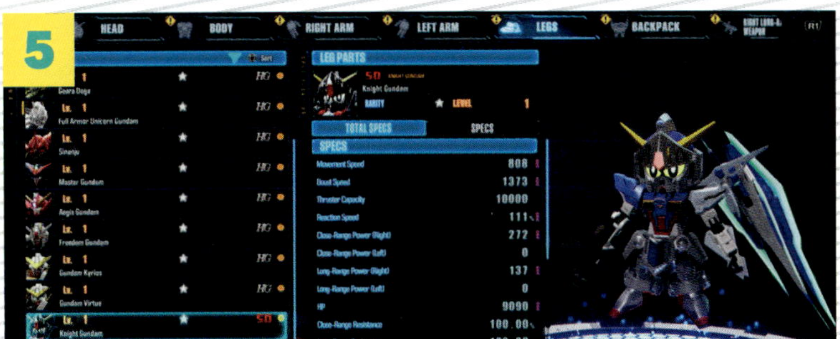

Play all the parts

■ It's always worth testing out a new part in your room before leaping into battle with it—or deciding it's not for you and leaving it to gather dust in your inventory. You'll get the most out of this game if you take the time to explore everything you collect.

Pac them in

■ Here's the collab you didn't know you needed in your life: a *Gundam Breaker* level based on *Pac-Man*. This creates a 3D version of the classic *Pac-Man* maze, complete with ghosts and power pills, and some awesome decals and stickers to collect!

FUNKO FUSION

Worlds collide in a funky fashion!

The Funko Pops range of bobblehead figurines will be familiar to anyone who's walked into a shop selling nerd stuff in the last ten years. Almost every figurine has the same basic shape—which has enabled Funko to produce a vast number of designs based on games, TV shows, movies, and real people! Almost anything you can think of has a Funko Pop version, so a franchise crossover video game was the inevitable next step.

FAST FACT

Funko was founded in 1998 by toy collector Mike Becker, who wanted to buy a coin bank of the mascot of the Big Boy restaurant chain—but when he couldn't get one, he licensed the rights to make his own!

UNIVERSAL SOLDIERS

■ Of course, there's no way they could fit every Funko into one game—not least because lots of different companies own all those properties. Just as *LEGO Dimensions* was mostly based around properties owned by Warner Bros. *Funko Fusion*'s pop culture figures are mostly drawn from things distributed by Universal Studios.

SETTING THE TONE

■ While the game is rated Teen and features family-friendly franchises like *Masters of the Universe* and *Crash Bandicoot*, the mix of properties means some—such as *Jaws*, *The Umbrella Academy*, and *Scott Pilgrim*—are aimed at a slightly older audience.

DINOSAURS, MAGIC, ART, AND CHICKEN

■ The clash of worlds is quite fun, as blockbusters like *Jurassic World* and *Wicked* rub shoulders with gaming franchises like *Five Nights at Freddy's* and *Mega Man*, but also artist Bob Ross from the 1980s instructional show *The Joy of Painting* and KFC's mascot Colonel Sanders.

TRANSFERABLE SKILLS

■ And as with *Dimensions*, the particular skills of a character from one world can be used in another—so if there's something you can't work out how to access, it may be that you need to unlock another character and come back later!

ANOTHER DIMENSION

■ The overall approach is a lot like *LEGO Dimensions* (though unlike that game, you don't get awesome minifigs in the pack): In pursuit of the evil Eddy Funko, you move between levels based in different worlds, solve some puzzles, and fight some bad guys.

LOONEY TUNES WACKY WORLD OF SPORTS

IN PERFECT TUNE, OR IN NEED OF A TUNE-UP?

Thanks to *Space Jam*, there's an enduring link between the *Looney Tunes* gang and sports. The tricky part of any game based on a cartoon is capturing the humor—too many of these games look right but don't feel right. *Wacky World of Sports* does a good job of this, with the current voice actors for the characters making everything sound authentic.

Fans of the original toons may be disappointed with the choice of 3D cell-shaded characters rather than 2D ones, but the environments are imaginative and each character's signature moves tie in well to their personalities, like Wile E. Coyote launching himself from a cannon. At times it really feels like you're playing a *Looney Tunes* cartoon!

QUICK TIPS

NINE TIMES NINE

When seeking to unlock all trophies, start with the Ultimate Cup, as it's the easiest mode. You need to win this nine times, and use nine different characters.

RISE TO THE CHALLENGE

Challenges is the next one you should go for, as this will unlock three special stadiums and you'll need them for the Sports Mode quests.

ENVIRONMENTAL AWARENESS

One of the Sports Mode quests is to trigger ten environment interactions in golf. After winning the game, start a round on hole 7 and hit the portal in the tent. Restart your round repeatedly until you have reached ten.

SPORTING CHANCES

There are no great surprises in the choice of sports here—the developers have gone for the ones that have reliably made good video games for decades.

BASKETBALL

This one was always a no-brainer, but sadly it's one of the less successful sports in the package—gameplay feels slow and, unusually for a cartoon sports game, and the AI feels unfairly overpowered!

SOCCER

This has a similar style to basketball and similar issues—its movement lacks the frantic feel of a cartoon, especially when you wind up to take a shot at goal.

TENNIS

Tennis usually makes for a great party game because it's so well suited to playing in teams of two—there's only local multiplayer in *Wacky World of Sports*, but this sport works really well.

GOLF

This is the most successful of the four sports. There's a reason we have crazy golf but not crazy tennis: It's just better suited to doing silly things, and dodging traps and spoiling opponents' shots is really fun.

FAST FACT

The name *Looney Tunes* was based on the title Disney used for their cartoon shorts, *Silly Symphony*. Warner Bros. cartoons were also often called *Merrie Melodies*, but that title hasn't stuck around!

LIKE THIS? TRY THIS:

LOONEY TUNES WORLD OF MAYHEM

The current version of this casual action RPG for mobile devices launched in 2018 and is still being supported with new events. It's simple stuff, but the characters are so well suited to the format; if you're a *Looney Tunes* fan, there's lots to enjoy here.

DRIVING GAMES

Driving games have always been a big part of the gaming world. The golden age of arcades saw Taito's *Speed Race*, Sega's *Monaco GP*, and Namco's *Pole Position* become high-grossing hits. Their emphasis on speed and realistic physics means they are often the first games to make use of advances in technology: They were some of the first to use 3D graphics, for instance. The polygon graphics of Namco's *Winning Run* and Sega's *Virtua Racing* were astonishing at the time.

As consoles became more powerful, they were able to match the realism seen in arcades. *Gran Turismo* became one of PlayStation's defining games when the original came out in 1997, and the series remains one of the most compelling reasons to buy a PlayStation over an Xbox. The series nailed the trickiest part of making a driving game: balancing realism with playability. Some gamers want everything to be accurate, others want it to be accessible and fun.

In recent years, the open-world driving game has shot up in popularity: The excellent *Forza Horizon* series now overshadows the series it was spun off from, *Forza Motorsport*. In this rundown of the latest titles, you'll see there are now many different angles a driving game can take. They continue to be popular with players too young to drive for real, those who wish they could do it at an elite level, and also those who just want to drive more dangerously than they ever would on a real road!

THE CHONKY BOYS: MONSTER JAM SHOWDOWN

The *Monster Jam* games have been chugging along since 2002, and *Showdown* is the ninth in the series. The crucial thing about a monster-truck game is the trucks have to feel like monster trucks: You want a sense of weight and power, and they should be a little difficult to handle, just like a real one. *Showdown* does that really well, but this is also a family-friendly game, so players can add some assist features if they're struggling.

THE BIGGEST OPEN WORLD: TEST DRIVE UNLIMITED SOLAR CROWN

The *Test Drive* series goes way back to 1987. The *Unlimited* subtitle was added in 2006 to indicate a move to an open-world map—they were doing it before *Forza Horizon*. But *Forza* has eaten their lunch, and so *Test Drive* is making a bigger lunch (maybe this is where the metaphor breaks down). Basically this is the most ambitious *Test Drive* yet, set on a full-size recreation of Hong Kong Island. While there's much to like about it, the fact there's no proper single-player option creates some frustrating issues.

A TRIP TO PARADISE: THE CREW MOTORFEST

The third game in *The Crew* series is a step up from previous games. *Motorfest* allows you to roam a couple of Hawaiian islands, taking part in a festival. It's heavily based around online multiplayer, but an offline mode was added after release. It's not going to knock *Forza Horizon* off its perch just yet, but it is emerging as a serious rival!

THE SCARY ONE: PACIFIC DRIVE

We've seen before survival games where you have to drive a car, but a full-on combo of survival game and driving game is more unusual. In *Pacific Drive* you're steering a station wagon through an area of the Pacific Northwest that's been walled off due to it being infested with horrors. The maintenance of your vehicle becomes crucial—it takes a beating, and you can't just call a mechanic or even buy the parts you need. If you can't fix it yourself, you're in trouble!

BEST ON SWITCH: HOT LAP RACING

With their emphasis on speed, detail, and realistic physics, driving games tend to focus on the more powerful PlayStation and Xbox platforms—leaving the poor old Switch short of sim-style driving games. Previously the best you could do was *GRID Autosport*, a part of a great Codemasters game from the PS3/Xbox 360 era—but *Hot Lap Racing* has finally stepped into the breach. It's no *Forza*, but it's got a nice variety of cars and styles, with plenty of licenses and a nice balance between sim and arcade.

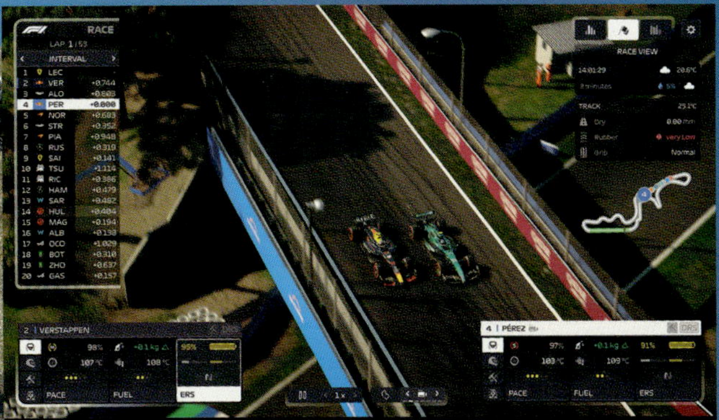

TAKING A BACK SEAT: F1 MANAGER 2024

The world's biggest motorsport competition has two official games—the main *F1* series is a solid part of the EA Sports stable, but Frontier Developments runs the separate *F1 Manager* series, which is one of the best sports management games out there. Managing a motorsports team just has so many aspects to it—as well as working with the drivers, you have a whole backroom staff to assemble and manage, and then there are all the components that go into the cars. One great idea in 2024's edition is the option to set your team's backstory—are you the plucky outsiders or the aggressive disruptors?

THE LONG HAUL: LE MANS ULTIMATE

There have been many attempts to bring the legendary Le Mans twenty-four-hour endurance race to video games, going right back to a 1976 arcade game by Atari. Nothing has quite matched up to the 1999 Sega Dreamcast classic *Le Mans 24 Hours*, though the circuit has featured in *Gran Turismo*, *iRacing*, and *Forza Motorsport*. But *Le Mans Ultimate* is a highly promising newcomer and features the other six circuits in the World Endurance Championship.

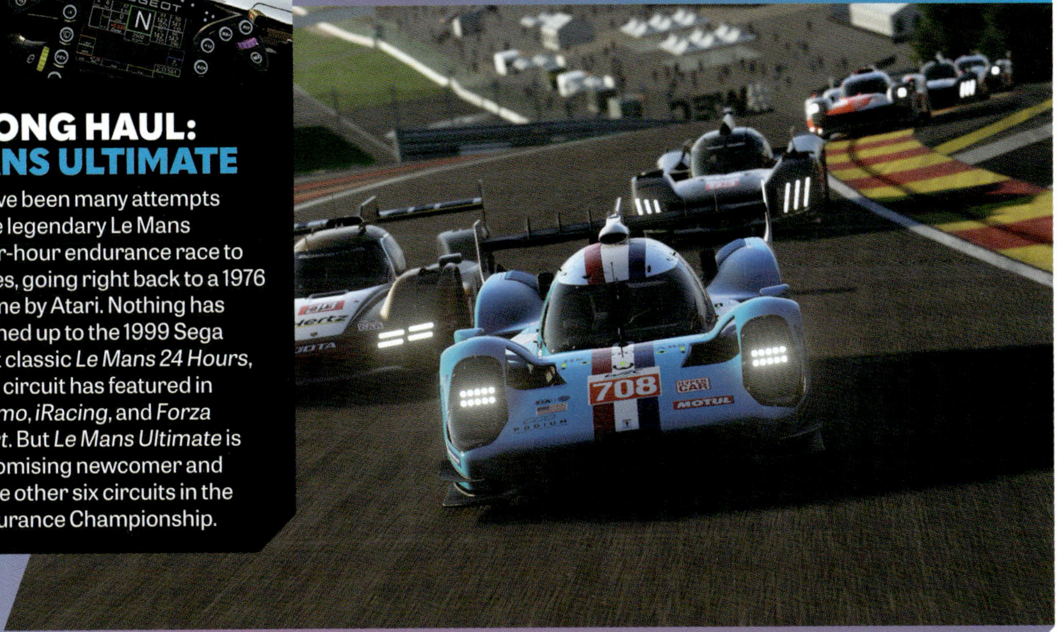

TAKING IT SLOW: EXPEDITIONS: A MUDRUNNER GAME

Driving games are all about speed, right? Wrong! In *Expeditions: A MudRunner Game* you head out on scientific expeditions, hauling equipment through treacherous environments. It's made by the creators of *SnowRunner* and *MudRunner*, and it takes you to some pretty spectacular locations in search of dinosaur fossils and significant ruins. But the lack of roads means the pace often slows to a crawl! It's a stiff challenge, and an unusual one.

OFF THE BEATEN TRACK: #DRIVE RALLY

There are some great rally games—Codemasters are doing superb work with the official *WRC* series—but they can be hardcore and offputting to newcomers. That's where *#DRIVE Rally* comes in. The rather silly hashtag title may belong to the twenty-first century, but this takes inspiration from simpler racing games from the 1990s, and indeed that's when it's set! Its colorful, chunky graphics are instantly appealing, and while it doesn't go for fully realistic handling, the cars drive really well. And it still provides a decent challenge—it's just not as punishing as the alternatives!

THE BIGGEST GARAGE: FORZA MOTORSPORT

The *Forza Motorsport* series was rebooted in 2023, and while its gameplay is on the more accessible side, visually it might be the most realistic racing game ever made. You can choose to get into the more technical details—or you can leave all that aside and just enjoy pure racing! Its real selling point is a huge range of cars and circuits, covering a range of different racing styles—it's a great all-arounder.

FREE TURISMO

While *Gran Turismo* still dominates the racing scene, it's not complacent about its position—at the end of 2024 *My First Gran Turismo* was released. It's essentially an extensive free demo version of *Gran Turismo 7* for PS4 and PS5. "Whether you're a parent introducing your family to racing or a longtime fan revisiting the series," says the description, "*My First Gran Turismo* captures the essence of those unforgettable first laps in a streamlined, approachable experience crafted especially for new players."

MIKA AND THE WITCH'S MOUNTAIN

A SWEET IDEA, BUT DOES IT DELIVER?

We've seen quite a few games lately that have been influenced by the movies of Studio Ghibli, but this has to be the most blatant. *Mika and the Witch's Mountain* follows aspiring witch Mika, who wants to go to witch school, but the harsh Grand Witch demands she prove herself by making her own way to the top of the mountain.

For this Mika needs a better broomstick, and for that she needs to earn money... So she takes a job as a courier in the village at the base of the mountain. This will feel very familiar to anyone who's seen (or even heard of) *Kiki's Delivery Service*. But hey, it's a great movie and a good premise for a game!

QUICK TIPS

VITAL STATS

Look out for the Napopo Statuettes that are scattered around the island—you'll need 100 of them to fully complete the game.

YOU'VE GOT TO URN IT

The tarot cards can be collected by cracking open urns from a height. Landing these is the trickiest part of the game, so line it up carefully!

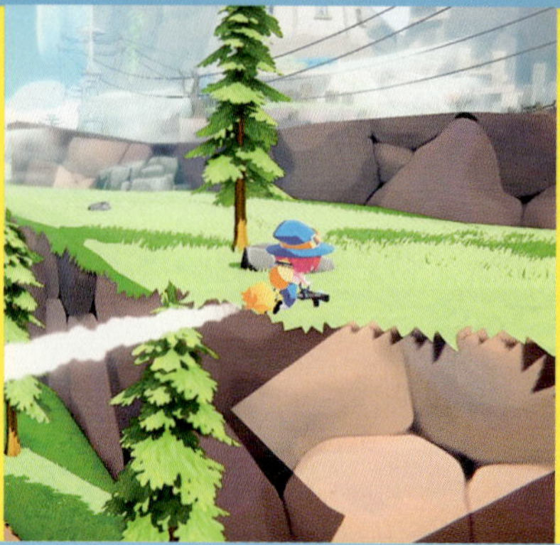

OSTRICH IN TIME

The three escaped baby ostriches are in these locations: the top of the tower in the Farmlands, the southwest corner of the Farmlands, and at the heart of the Factory Mine.

WITCH WAY?

Mika and the Witch's Mountain is a fairly simple game based on exploring the island where the titular mountain is located, earning money, and finding collectibles.

STAMP OF APPROVAL

In order to get paid, you don't just have to deliver each parcel, you also have to make sure it doesn't get damaged or wet. A good delivery gets you a green stamp.

BOOK A REDELIVERY

Crashing into a wall will damage the parcel, but this isn't too hard to avoid, either, as the flying controls are smooth and responsive. You can easily retry a failed delivery.

SURFACE TENSION

Don't worry too much about the pitfalls. You might think skimming the surface of the water will get the parcel wet, but it doesn't—as long as you stay on your broomstick, it's fine.

SIDE SPIN

The deliveries can get repetitive after a while, and there's more fun and challenge in side quests where you find items on the island and have to work out who they belong to!

FAST FACT

Mika and the Witch's Mountain was codeveloped by Nukefist, whose next game, Genokids, is a hack-and-slash adventure about a rock group battling an alien invasion.

LIKE THIS? TRY THIS:

POSTKNIGHT 2

This neat, casual RPG, available for iOS, Android, and Windows, sees you joining a delivery crew in a fantasy realm called Prism, battling monsters and meeting a range of cool characters.

PALIA

FARMING WITH STRANGERS IN A STRANGE LAND!

There are lots of familiar elements in *Palia*. It's based around farming and village life, with mechanics you'll have seen in *Stardew Valley* and *Animal Crossing*. The way it's divided into home and town areas and you randomly landing in a server with other players when you log in, feels like a more developed version of Roblox MMOs such as *Adopt Me!* And overall, the world and the quest system feels like a low-stakes version of *Breath of the Wild*.

Palia launched in open beta on Windows and Switch in 2023, and its developers have been making tweaks and improvements ever since, building a welcoming and enthusiastic community along the way. If they can get it right, a cozy fantasy farming freemium MMO sounds like it could be huge!

QUICK TIPS

GLIDE AWAY

Speak to Jina to progress the Ancient Battery quests—these will ultimately unlock the glider for you, which is very handy!

BREAKING CAMP

Don't bother furnishing your tent any more than you need to progress the quests because after that you'll be taking it down to build a house.

FISHING SCAM

Once you've learned to fish, it's a quick way to earn money. The fishing pools contain higher quality fish, which are worth more.

OPEN BORDERS

After creating and naming an avatar, you materialize in a world inhabited by the elf-like Majiri. How you got there is a mystery, but they help you settle in.

GET AROUND TOWN

There are lots of aspects to life here and lots of people to learn about them from. They're spread out across Kilima Village, so always speak to the nearest one—you don't want to be crisscrossing the village looking for them all!

GO YOUR OWN WAY

Palia is combat-free, and while following the quests means you'll unlock things quicker, you can focus on your favorite areas, whether that's building relationships with NPCs or working to improve your home.

SWITCHING SCREENS

The game supports cross-progression between different platforms—so while you may want to explore on your Switch, you can move to the PC to use the keyboard to chat with the real people you meet.

THAT'S MINE

Gathering resources and building items has a *Minecraft* feel—your inventory is at the bottom of the screen. You use the right trigger to swing your axe or pick, and you make stuff at a crafting table.

FAST FACT

***Palia*'s future was in doubt during 2024, as its developer, Singularity 6, was forced to make big cuts to its staff—but fortunately the company was bought by Daybreak, which runs *Dungeons & Dragons Online* and *Lord of the Rings Online*.**

LIKE THIS? TRY THIS:

WYLDE FLOWERS

Another farm sim with a fantasy twist, *Wylde Flowers* sees you playing as an aspiring witch. It's got a heavier narrative than other farm sims, but you can choose your pace if you don't want it to pass too quickly.

TOP 10 CITY SIMS

Excitement is building!

For decades, the city-sim scene was synonymous with *SimCity*. The revolutionary first game was followed by increasingly detailed sequels, along with spin-offs like *The Sims*—before the disastrous 2013 reboot, which seemingly sunk the franchise for good. But the city sim lives on, and developers have put their own spins on it—crossing it over with other genres and taking it to other worlds. Here are ten of the best!

10 The Wandering Village

A pretty straightforward and low-key take on the city-sim genre, with one important difference: You build your town on the back of an enormous beast known as Onbu. This adds an extra dimension as you must manage your citizens as well as Onbu, guiding it and making sure it gets enough rest and food.

AVAILABLE ON: Xbox Series S/X, Xbox One, PC, Mac

09 Manor Lords

Medieval city builders are a popular subgenre, and often include combat and strategy elements. One of the great things about *Manor Lords* is how it gives you the option to focus on building or warfare, or a mix of both. It's also one of the most realistic city sims, with six different types of taxation and environmental factors including deforestation having an effect. The ability to step into your town and walk around is a great touch!

AVAILABLE ON: PC

08 SteamWorld Build

The post-apocalypse *SteamWorld* series is unusual: The games share the same Old West setting but have covered several different genres, from strategy and RPG to metroidvania. *SteamWorld Build* is mostly a city-sim game, but it also has a dungeon-crawling element—you search abandoned mineshafts for technology that will help your city progress further. And while many city sims have no particular goal to work toward, here you can collect rocket parts to help you escape the planet!

AVAILABLE ON: **Nintendo Switch, PS5, PS4, Xbox Series S/X, Xbox One, PC**

07 Surviving Mars

There have been plenty of space-based city sims, and *Surviving Mars* makes it clear that colonizing another planet isn't as easy as some people make out! You're presented with plenty of problems as you set up home on the red planet: As well as building the habitat, you need to keep your citizens provided with oxygen, protect them against disasters, and also search for fertile terrain.

AVAILABLE ON: **PS5, PS4, Xbox Series S/X, Xbox One, PC, Mac**

06 Farthest Frontier

Another medieval-themed game, *Farthest Frontier* offers an amazing level of detail. Its farming mechanics feel really realistic, and you can't casually stack up resources—food will go bad if it's not eaten, so you need to plan your harvests carefully! One thing's for sure, you'll come out of it glad you live in a world with supermarkets and fridge freezers!

AVAILABLE ON: **PC**

05 Timberborn

■ It's the future. Humans are extinct. Who's building cities now? Beavers! This is a city sim like no other, with an emphasis on directing and conserving water to protect against droughts. You can choose your approach—do you want to be one of the technology-focused Iron Teeth beavers or the organically minded Folktails? And as you build a new world, can you do a better job of it than humanity did?

AVAILABLE ON: PC, Mac

04 Townscaper

■ City-sim games can be stressful, with citizens making demands, more options than you can keep track of, and disasters blindsiding you. *Townscaper* is a much more relaxed take on the genre, with a simplified user interface and a creative sandbox approach. Developer Oskar Stålberg has said it's more like a toy than a game: You just create clusters of buildings on an infinite sea for as long as you like. It looks great and is strangely addictive!

AVAILABLE ON: Nintendo Switch, PC, iOS, Android

03 Anno 1800

■ The *Anno* games are set in different eras, and the seventh in the series follows the futuristic *Anno 2070* and *Anno 2205* by returning to the historical settings of previous games. As you can probably guess, this one takes place in the nineteenth century. Part of the challenge of these games is getting to grips with how things work in each game's era—what resources are available and what's possible with the technology level. We're in the early Industrial Age here, so factories and overseas trade are all-important.

AVAILABLE ON: PS5, Xbox Series S/X, PC

02 Against the Storm

Against the Storm is an excellent hybrid of city sim and roguelike. It's set in the Smoldering City, the only safe haven from the eternally raging Blightstorm: You take the role of Queen's Viceroy and between visitations from the storm, you must rebuild the villages around the city. The storm will come again and trash what you've built, but you will have unlocked things that help you build the next one. This adds a level of stress beyond other city sims, but it also gives you a clear goal to work toward!

AVAILABLE ON: PC

01 Cities: Skylines

If you want a contemporary take on the *SimCity* experience, it really has to be *Cities: Skylines*. The original game arrived at the perfect moment to step into the gap created by the collapse of *SimCity*, and it offers everything you'd expect from a modern city-building game while also being accessible to newcomers. The sequel has had some growing pains, so until they work those out we suggest sticking with the original or remastered versions.

AVAILABLE ON: Nintendo Switch, PS5, PS4, Xbox Series S/X, Xbox One, PC, Mac

SNUFKIN: MELODY OF MOOMINVALLEY

STAYING IN TUNE WITH NATURE!

The Moomins are a family of trolls (even though they look like cute hippos) created by the Finnish writer/artist Tove Jansson. The books are beloved by millions across the world for their mix of gentle whimsy and melancholy weirdness, and the characters have also featured in movies and TV shows. The ones that have worked well have avoided being too flashy or modern—it just doesn't suit them—and bringing them to video games has proved tricky. The most notable previous *Moomins* game—the Game Boy Color *Moomin's Tale*—was a generic action platformer.

So, *Snufkin: Melody of Moominvalley* really came out of nowhere! This musical adventure captures the charm of the original stories in a way previous games just didn't.

QUICK TIPS

BE A HOARDER

Most of the quests involve collecting things, so think ahead and collect everything as you go along. The game rewards you for interacting with its world!

SOUND DECISION

Don't play this game with the sound off! Listening helps you to play. You can hear hidden inspiration, which saves you spending time searching.

BUILD YOURSELF UP

At some point you'll need more stamina to be able to get away—find Muskrat near Moominhouse and he'll increase your stamina meter.

TIME OF THE SEASON

The main character of *Snufkin: Melody of Moominvalley* isn't a Moomin at all. Snufkin is the best friend of the series' central character, Moomintroll, and while the Moomins hibernate in winter, Snufkin moves around with the seasons.

WATERCOLOR WORLD

This is a stunningly beautiful game! It shows how advanced graphics can be about more than making everything photorealistic. You feel like you've stepped into a storybook, with soft watercolor backdrops.

ON THE MOVE

Snufkin is off on his wanderings as the game opens. The plot is inspired by part of the book *Moominsummer Madness*, in which Snufkin seeks revenge on a grumpy park keeper.

KEEP ON THE GRASS

Snufkin is outraged to learn Moominvalley has been turned into neat, orderly parks and wants to restore them to nature. This gives the action a nicely anarchic edge, as you rip up signs and topple statues.

SIGHTS TO BEHOLD

There are points in the game where you can interact with the scenery and take in a view. These don't help your progress, but appreciating the world around you is the point of the game—so do it!

FAST FACT

There were nine Moomin novels, starting with *The Moomins and the Great Flood* in 1945 and ending with *Moominvalley in November* in 1970. There are two Moomin theme parks—one in Finland and one in Japan.

LIKE THIS? TRY THIS:

THE ARTFUL ESCAPE

This indie platform game also uses a musical mechanic, as the rock 'n' roll loving nephew of a folk music legend goes on a weird quest and engages in guitar battles. A rather different vibe from *Snufkin*, but it also looks amazing!

MAKING MELODIES IN MOOMINVALLEY

How music helps you unlock Snufkin's world!

Moomin creator Tove Jansson was very critical of any versions of her stories that featured guns or excessive violence, and so the designers of *Snufkin: Melody of Moominvalley* were keen to find a nonviolent approach. They hit upon using Snufkin's music as a way of interacting with the world.

1

Inflicting harmonica

■ The first instrument Snufkin makes use of is his harmonica, which charms creatures into helping. You learn how to use this early in the game, as you convince the friendly sea creature to carry you across the river. But for some creatures, you'll need to build up inspiration from quivering bushes before you can charm them with music.

2

Bird brains

■ The harmonica can also be used to charm the blackbirds you run into along the way. They may be the solution to a puzzle, like when you need to save Sniff: The bird will scare the spider away. You can also use blackbirds to fetch inspiration you can't otherwise reach.

FAST FACT

A DLC expansion for the game—*Fuddler's Courtship*—was released in December 2024, and follows Snufkin's friend Fuddler as he tries to win the heart of Snufkin's half-sister Mymble.

3 Bee musical

■ The flute, which you acquire later in the game, tends to have a calming effect. It can be used to get rid of bees—just target the bee while using the flute—and to send red weed creatures to sleep. Later you can use it to turn alligators and snakes into platforms.

4 First raft choice

■ A major quest in the game involves building a raft that takes you to Hattifatteners Island. You can take the game at your own pace and do side quests, but completing the island quests unlocks the full soundtrack! We recommend focusing on this goal first, as it enhances the whole game.

The Arctic Circle

■ The Moomins are from Finland, and Hyper Games, the studio that made the game, is in Norway. The Nordic connection continues in the music, as the soundtrack features the Icelandic group Sigur Rós. Tracks from their album have been included alongside new pieces by game soundtrack composer Oda Tilset.

5 Drum up some inspiration

■ The third instrument, the drum, is acquired from the Hemulen Plant Collector on Hattifatteners Island. This can get rid of blockages—and it can also flatten down the ferns that slow your pace and may contain inspiration. You may want to leave these fern-heavy areas to explore after you pick up the drum!

PENNY'S BIG BREAKAWAY

IT'S AN ACTION PLATFORMER WITH STYLE, YO!

Anyone who's played the 1990s *Sonic* games will immediately find something familiar about *Penny's Big Breakaway*—all those bold, shiny secondary colors make you feel like you're back in Spring Yard Zone. So it's not a shock to learn one of the directors on this was Christian Whitehead, previously responsible for the excellent *Sonic Mania*.

The *Sonic* feel extends to the gameplay, which is speedy, inventive, and involves lots of leaping and bouncing around. You play as Penny, a street performer who possesses a yo-yo with cosmic string. At a talent show audition, Yo-Yo has stolen Emperor Eddie's pants, so Penny is now avoiding the emperor's mobs of penguin guards…

QUICK TIPS

C'MON, BOUNCE!

■ There are a number of Yo-Yo moves the game doesn't teach you! Throw Yo-Yo and hold the button to keep it out, then try jumping on it—you can bounce off the top.

UP YOU GO

■ You can wall bounce by jumping into a wall and then away from it—but to get more height, fire Yo-Yo a moment before you hit the wall. You'll bounce off Yo-Yo and upward!

RIDE ON UP

■ The Ride button can be charged up to give you an extra burst of speed—just hold it down. This also works when you're in the air if you want to hit the ground with a speed burst.

STRING THEM ALONG

Yo-Yo is a weapon, a vehicle, and a reach extender all in one. Penny can ride it like a chariot, spin it around like a hammer, use it to break things, and flip switches . . .

GETTING INTO THE SWING

Penny can also make Yo-Yo freeze in the air briefly and swing from it. You need to practice your jump-and-swing timing, because there are plenty of areas where you can fall to your death!

STICKING TO A VIEWPOINT

The right thumbstick is used for Yo-Yo—you need it when spinning—so you can't move the camera. This can be frustrating with delicate jumps and when searching for items!

LOCAL KNOWLEDGE

Just as *Sonic* got even more fun when you knew the layout of a level and could take it at high speed, in this game it's worth revisiting levels to see if you can play them with more style.

KILLER COMBOS

The rewards you get for putting together combos are a clue: Learn to combine Penny's tricks and the game opens up. This is what makes the game special! You can also show off your tricks at the end of a stage.

FAST FACT

There's archaeological evidence that yo-yos have existed since at least 440 BCE, as an ancient Greek urn exists with a picture of a boy playing with one on the side.

LIKE THIS? TRY THIS:

FREEDOM PLANET 2

The *Freedom Planet* games are also *Sonic*-influenced platformers, and the second in the series improves on the first. It's got a more retro style than *Penny*, but it's a huge and well-designed game!

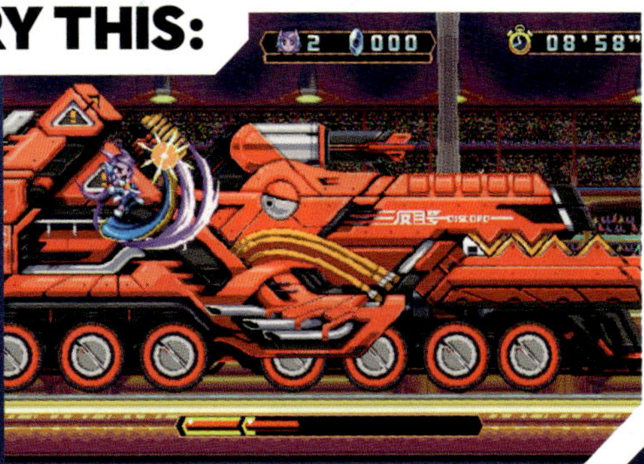

Duck Detective: The Secret Salami

Looking for a mystery adventure? This fits the bill!

■ This homage to classic hard-boiled mystery fiction replaces the usual wisecracking private detective with . . . a duck. Private eye Eugene McQuacklin is hired to come to an office building and investigate the case of a stolen lunch (the salami mentioned in the title), but quickly learns the place is full of bitter rivalries and festering grudges. McQuacklin must pick his way through it all. It's definitely on the cozy side, and offers a moderate level of challenge. You can treat it like a movie, playing through it all in one sitting—maybe even get friends and family to watch and make suggestions!

Memory hole

■ There are so many brilliant ideas in this, and they start with the tutorial, which takes the form of McQuacklin working out what happened to him last night. Investigations are done the usual way in mystery games—speaking to people and searching for clues.

Tracing paper

The graphics are instantly appealing, with great character design and a simple animation style that's reminiscent of *Paper Mario*, with its "cutout" white outlines. The voice acting adds a lot to the experience, too—but you need to pay attention to the highlighted words…

Drawing a blank

There's an in-game notebook that uses a similar mechanic to the indie mystery game *Case of the Golden Idol*. Finding the right highlighted words from the dialogue and inserting them into the correct blanks in your notebook builds the case.

FAST FACT

For those wanting more McQuacklin, he returns to take on a supernatural case at a haunted campsite in *Duck Detective: The Ghost of Glamping*.

Hit the right note

But wait, surely you can just throw the words in randomly until they fit? Well, the game won't tell you which words you've got wrong on each page—so it's quicker to just investigate, and more entertaining, too.

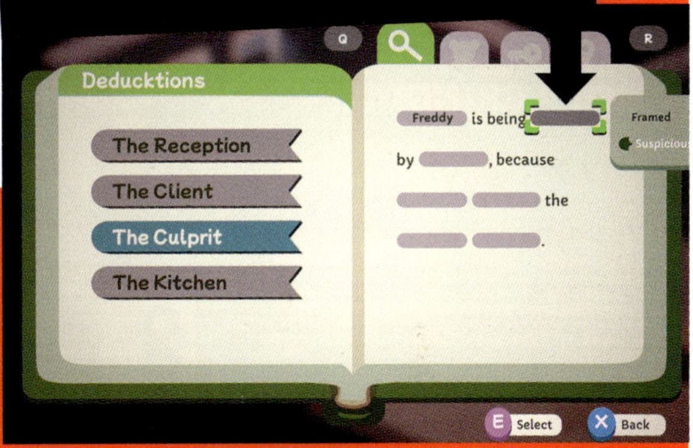

Short but sweet

You can play through the mystery in about three hours, so it goes quickly, and mystery games don't have much replay value. But weigh that against how much it costs (not much) and how much fun you'll have playing it (lots).

PEPPER GRINDER

THIS GAME IS DEFINITELY NOT A GRIND!

One of the best games on the Game Boy Advance was *Drill Dozer*, in which a young woman called Jill used a large drill to fight enemies and explore her world. *Pepper Grinder* takes that concept and runs with it. Its heroine is Pepper, a pirate who prefers finding treasure to stealing it, whose hoard has been stolen by Narlings. But she's found a drill called Grinder, and she's going to use it to get her treasure back.

The result is a classic 2D platformer with speedy, exciting gameplay, incredibly clever level design, and appealing retro graphics. It keeps offering up surprises and challenges, and you'll find it hard to stop playing once you start!

QUICK TIPS

STICK TO THE STICK

■ You can use the directional buttons to move, but you really need to use an analog stick to get the movement right. If you're playing on Steam, use a controller!

A MOMENT'S GRACE

■ After walking off a ledge, you can still jump during the first split second of your fall. This can make tricky jumps a little easier.

SURFACE TENSION

■ The ideal moment to dash while drilling is when you're about to reach the surface—you'll get the greatest distance this way.

DRILL INTO IT

The brilliance of *Pepper Grinder* is its simplicity. It's like *Sonic the Hedgehog* in how movement and attack are linked—Grinder is Pepper's weapon, but it also allows her to dig for treasure and travel through soft ground.

DRILL AND DASH

There are only two controls—right trigger to drill, B to jump and also to dash while drilling, and you need to use them together. Reflexes and timing are all-important!

FLIPPING OUT

The game also changes up the challenge regularly, so it's never repetitive. For instance, when you flip one of the hatches in this image, they all flip—so you have to find the route that ends with the final hatch open.

CONTROL FREAK

It's hard to control Pepper when she's drilling, but the movement is perfect, and it never gets too frustrating. When you nail a section and sail smoothly through, it feels really exciting!

ROCK HARD

This isn't a long game, but it's a tricky one! You'll die a few times before you get past some sections, and trial and error is needed on others.

FAST FACT

Drill Dozer **was made by Game Freak, the developers behind the** ***Pokémon*** **games—in fact, it's the only non-Pokémon game they made during the whole of the 2000s.**

LIKE THIS? TRY THIS:

SUPER MEAT BOY

If *Pepper Grinder* whets your appetite for a real challenge, take on the notoriously tough—but also ingenious and funny—*Super Meat Boy*, one of the best 2D platformers out there!

MARVEL 1943: RISE OF HYDRA

Superheroes and hyperrealism!

The latest game to feature the Marvel superheroes takes place against a very real, and very serious, historical backdrop. Set in Nazi-occupied Paris during World War II—as well as other locations around the world—it stars Captain America, but also the Black Panther of that era, T'Challa's grandfather, Azzuri! As you can see from this picture, the two heroes start off at loggerheads but soon unite to fight the true enemy. "It's pretty black and white," says development head Amy Hennig. "Who doesn't want to punch a Nazi?"

WAR ON TWO FRONTS

As well as the Nazis, our gang of four must also face off against Hydra, who are operating in the shadows. Wakanda itself also features in the game, as its people—who usually don't get involved in the wider world—accept they can't stay neutral in this war.

SPIES AND SOLDIERS

The game's core cast of playable characters is filled out by Wakandan spymaster Nanali and US soldier Gabriel Jones, a member of the Howling Commandos. The gameplay shifts as you switch between the different characters.

FAST FACT

The Howling Commandos appeared in a Marvel Comics series that began in 1963 and was set during WWII. The squadron was led by future S.H.I.E.L.D. commander Nick Fury, in his first-ever comics appearance!

ALMOST HUMAN

Amy Hennig says Epic Games' MetaHuman capture technology was essential. "We really wanted the visual fidelity to be high so that you could kind of forget that you're looking at a game, that it should feel and look and sound and smell like you're watching a great Marvel movie or TV show, but you're driving the action."

UFO 50

NOT JUST A GAME, BUT A *WORLD* OF GAMES!

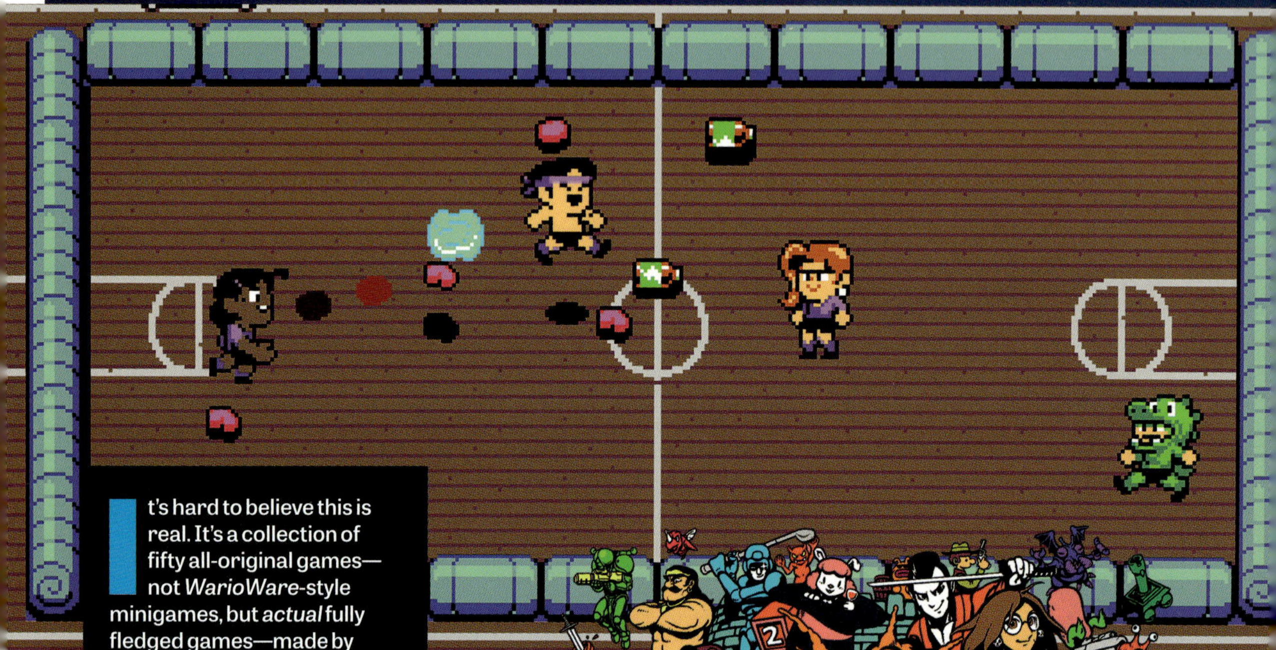

It's hard to believe this is real. It's a collection of fifty all-original games—not *WarioWare*-style minigames, but *actual* fully fledged games—made by a team of designers led by Derek Yu (creator of the indie hit *Spelunky*) and Jon Perry. They put these together over nine years in between other projects, and it grew into the concept of a fictional games company from the 1980s called UFO Soft collecting their entire output. However, the creators felt it was more important to have gameplay that works for a modern audience rather than be totally faithful to 8-bit gaming.

The variety on offer is wild—sports games, puzzle games, shoot-'em-ups, and classic platformers, often with some unusual twist. From *Grimstone*, a Wild West JRPG which takes around sixty hours to complete, to the golf-themed metroidvania *Golfaria*, it's all here!

QUICK TIPS

TOWERING GENIUS

If you enter EXEC-MIAS you'll unlock the secret fifty-first game (because fifty weren't enough)—*Miasma Tower*, in which you explore the UFO Soft offices.

SPEAKING IN CODE

Cheat codes include PLAY-FAIR for *Hot Foot* (allows you to draft any player), BENS-MODE for *Mortol* (150 lives), FORE-EVER for *Golfaria* (unlimited strokes), MAKE-GLEE for *Party House* (unlocks shop customizer), and ALFA-BEST for *Velgress* (all upgrades granted).

SETTING YOUR TERMINAL

There's a terminal you can use to enter cheat codes—just be aware you won't be able to unlock House Gifts or Trophies when using them (which is fair enough), and saving will be disabled.

OPTION PARALYSIS

There's so much in *UFO 50*, most players aren't going to get to the end of every game. In fact, it can be hard to know where to start! But here are four we recommend…

MINI & MAX

This platformer is all set in one room—Mini and her dog, Max, shrink down and have adventures at the micro level as they try to find a way out.

ELFAZAR'S HAT

This one's a scrolling shoot-'em-up in the classic arcade style, similar to the SNES game *Pocky & Rocky*, and it's also one of the best co-op games in the collection.

PORGY

A superb metroidvania that sees you exploring an underwater world in a yellow submarine, trying to conserve fuel and searching for fuel tanks that will enable you to expand your range.

VALBRACE

This game is a great dungeon-crawling action RPG with super-limited animation and real-time combat. Look out for the Bouncy Ball sometimes dropped by the Jesters when defeated—it's actually a good weapon!

FAST FACT

To make it look like all the games in *UFO 50* were made for the same 1980s consoles (the LX-I, LX-II, and LX-III), they all used the same palette of just thirty-two colors.

LIKE THIS? TRY THIS:

NINTENDO WORLD CHAMPIONSHIPS: NES EDITION

If *UFO 50* inspires you to go back to the source, this Switch game—inspired by the Nintendo World Championship events that began in 1990—creates challenges out of classic NES games like *Kirby's Adventure*, *Super Mario Bros.*, *Metroid*, and *The Legend of Zelda*.

Rusty Rabbit

Bringing new meaning to going down the rabbit hole!

We all had our own ways of coping with the COVID-19 lockdowns. Gen Urobuchi, anime screenwriter (he created *Puella Magi Madoka Magica*) and visual novel creator, decided to play around with the Unity engine to make a game. For fun. "It was purely a hobby," he said.

In the original version, you played as a mech suit with a normal white rabbit sitting in the driver's seat. But the game kept on expanding, to the point where Urobuchi wanted to do something with it. "So I showed my demo to the folks at [publisher] NetEase, and they said, 'How about we remake this idea in Unreal Engine and turn it into a sellable product?'" So that's what they did!

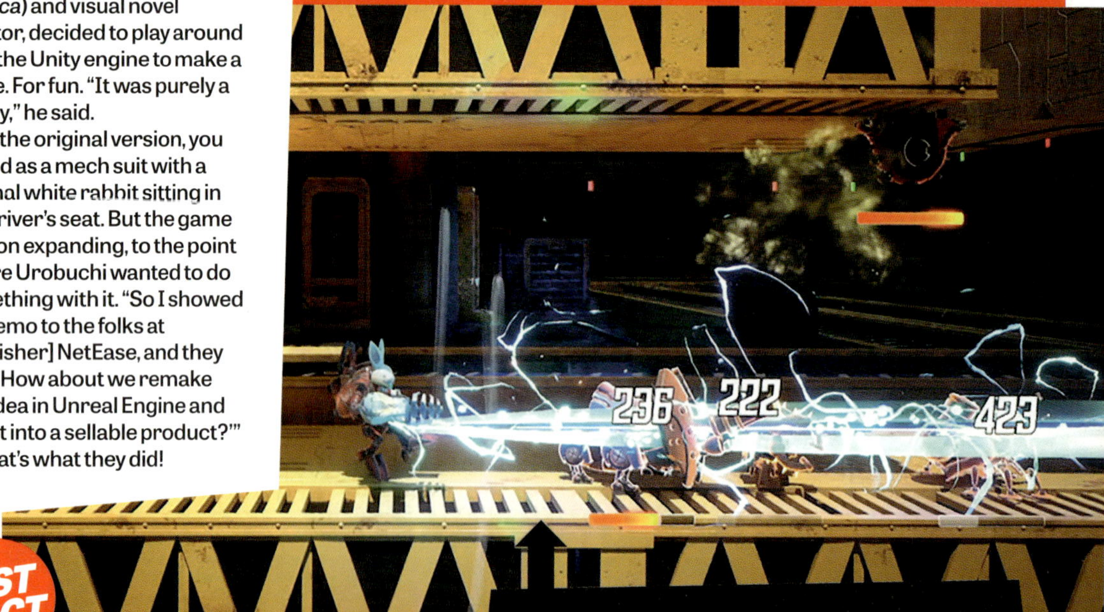

FAST FACT

Gen Urobuchi wrote the screenplays for a trilogy of animated *Godzilla* movies—*Planet of the Monsters*, *City on the Edge of Battle*, and *The Planet Eater*—and the 2022 Netflix movie *Bubble*.

Rise of the rabbits

Rusty Rabbit takes place on an Earth that was abandoned by humanity thousands of years ago. (Those lockdown vibes might have had an influence on this.) The world is now dominated by rabbits like Stamp, who is reckless, middle-aged, and makes a living as a "rust digger," foraging for scrap in his mech suit.

St. Peter

■ Stamp is more humanoid than the white rabbit from the demo. There's a lot of humor in the game, as you might expect. The rabbit civilization believes it's the rightful dominant species of Earth because they've read *Peter Rabbit* and treat it as we do the Bible!

Berry brave

■ Stamp joins the Blackberry Corps, or the BBs—a team of rust diggers trying to go deeper into the sacred ruin known as Smokestack Mountain. His hunting turns up what seems to be information about his daughter, whom he hasn't seen in a very long time—and it suggests she might be in trouble.

Get clued up

■ Stamp embarks on a search for further clues, looking for the ancient D-TAM computer terminals that store this information—and the other six BBs have a part to play, too. It's a Metroidvania—you progress by upgrading Stamp's mech suit back at your home base and then heading out again.

Slightly random

■ However, Urobuchi also wanted some roguelike sections. So while the "story" dungeons are in his words "more linear and contain RPG elements," there are also optional dungeons that are randomly generated. The result certainly looks a lot better than the games we threw together in Roblox during lockdown!

TOP 10 MOBILE GAMES

Here are some top picks for gaming on the go . . .

A lot of the best new mobile games have been RPGs, with many different styles represented, ranging from a seriously challenging deck builder to one where you can assemble a team of Disney heroes. But there's also some brilliant creativity on display in other genres!

10 Disney Pixel RPG

This is another attempt by Disney to do something interesting with their core characters (see also the *Epic Mickey* remaster on pages 88–89), and it's a good one. It uses simplified turn-based action, where each character has only three actions, so battles don't drag on, and even those who've never played an RPG before can get involved. And it's lots of fun putting together a team of characters from different Disney worlds!

AVAILABLE ON: Android

09 Monument Valley 3

The *Monument Valley* puzzle games have been big hits thanks to their striking design and relaxing vibes. With *Monument Valley 3*, the series moved to Netflix's games platform—all three are now exclusive to Netflix—and while it doesn't hit the heights of previous games, it's well worth playing. Its world is crumbling while the waters are rising, and a major new feature is the ability to sail a boat around it!

AVAILABLE ON: Android

08 Scattered Verse

OK, so this is a game about appreciating poetry, and . . . Wait, come back! It may sound like a worthy educational game, but *Scattered Verse* is a superbly designed platformer where you collect letters to put lines of poetry back together, with each environment reflecting the subject of the poem. There's something really satisfying about slotting the letters into place, and all the stages are enjoyable to spend time in.

AVAILABLE ON: **iOS, Android**

07 Pokémon Trading Card Game Pocket

There are so many deck-building mobile games, it was only a matter of time before *Pokémon*—perhaps the biggest name in deck-building card games—got in on the act. It offers the fun of collecting and playing with *Pokémon* cards without the huge expenditure, and it's easier to learn how to play the game in digital form, with tutorials and an option to auto-build your deck from the cards you own.

AVAILABLE ON: **iOS, Android**

06 Caves of Lore

Mobile gamers have been well supplied with turn-based RPGs with retro graphics, but *Caves of Lore* is an especially good one. It's well written and has plenty of variety. The quest into the caves is prompted by the Calamity, a fog that has caused everyone to lose their memories. Be warned—there aren't a lot of hints in this game, so you have to work it out for yourself!

AVAILABLE ON: **Android (also PC and Mac)**

05 Hidden Through Time 2: Myths & Magic

■ This is a typical hidden-object game with a relaxed, meditative style, set in eras from Ancient Greece to the 1980s—but it's also got a smart extra element, where you can choose to view the scene at different times, which means different weather conditions. Some objects are only visible at one time, some are only visible at the other—so you need to check both to find everything! Steam users can make and submit their own levels.

AVAILABLE ON: iOS, Android (also Nintendo Switch, PS5, Xbox Series S/X, PC, Mac)

04 Ex Astris

■ Yes, this RPG in which you play an investigator sent from Earth to an alien world is confusing. You may often have no idea what's going on. But that's not a problem, because *Ex Astris* is so well designed in other ways. Combat is great, with all kinds of factors that can affect your characters, driving you to keep exploring and finding new things to add into the mix. And if the idea was to simulate the experience of going to an alien planet and not understanding anything, then job done!

AVAILABLE ON: iOS, Android

03 Wildfrost

■ Roguelike deck-builder games (where the world and foes are randomly generated as you go along) are another popular phone genre, and if you're a fan of them, you have to give *Wildfrost* a try. It tasks you with vanquishing a mysterious frost that has taken over the land. Despite its cute and colorful appearance, this is a tough game to beat, and one with real tactical depth. It's free to try, and you pay a premium to unlock the full game.

AVAILABLE ON: iOS, Android (also Nintendo Switch, Xbox Series S/X, Xbox One, PC, Mac)

02 Crash Course Builder

■ This combination of kart racing game and rhythm game is ingenious. The shape of each course changes with the music, so you have to move to the beat in order to complete each course. But the game's designers, Australian studio Wombat Brawler, wanted a course designer to be at the center of the game (that's why it's in the title), so players can make the courses as easy or as difficult as they like!

AVAILABLE ON: iOS, Android (also PC, Mac)

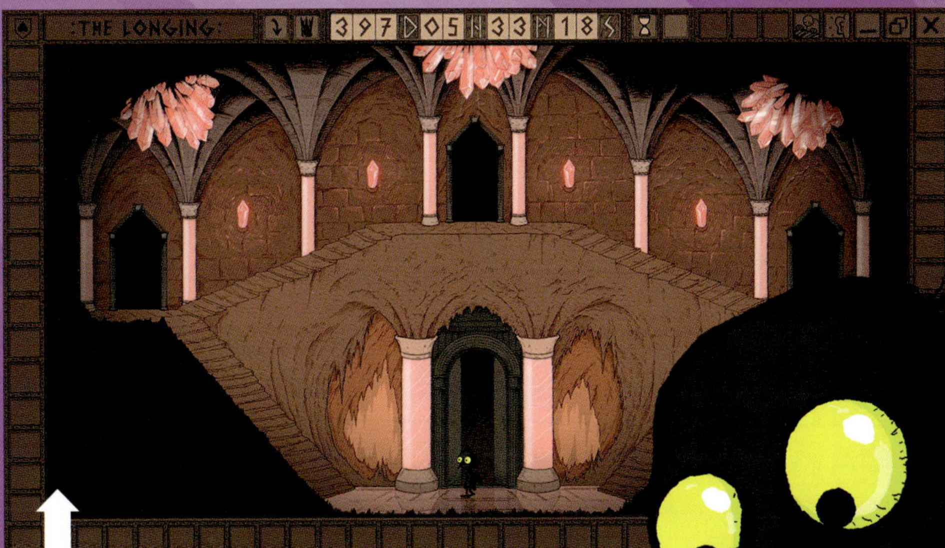

01 The Longing

■ This is a strange idea, but it really works—a cross between an adventure and an idle game that's designed to be played over 400 IRL days. You play as a Shade who's been tasked with waking your king at the end of his 400-day sleep in a network of caves. You're free to roam in the meantime, as long as you don't leave the caves. Some doors will make you wait days or weeks for them to open. It sounds dull and frustrating, but it's the opposite—the discoveries are exciting and it makes you see life differently!

AVAILABLE ON: iOS, Android (also Nintendo Switch, PC, Mac)

INFINITY NIKKI

VISUAL NOVEL SERIES ENTERS WORLD WITHOUT LIMITS!

The popular *Nikki* series of mobile games started in 2012, and with *Infinity Nikki*, the fifth in the series, it made the jump to other platforms, with PS5 and Windows versions also available from the day of release. And whereas previous games fitted their stories around dressing up and having style battles, *Infinity Nikki* is bigger and more ambitious.

Competitive styling is still an important element, but *Infinity Nikki* is an open-world adventure aiming to compete with the likes of *Genshin Impact*. Like *Genshin*, it's free to play and makes its money from tempting players into splashing out on gacha pulls. Thanks to the huge number of collectible clothing items (there are thousands), there's enough to keep players going for a long time!

QUICK TIPS

IN THE MAIN

There's a definite benefit to focusing on the main story before doing side quests and random exploration because it unlocks areas and enables you to acquire Ability Outfits.

BE A HOARDER

Collect everything you can. Once you have an item, you can track it and find more—and collecting also unlocks special design sketches in the Heart of Infinity.

BLING IT ON

Always target enemies carrying large red bags—those are full of Bling! Hit them three times and you can take them down and grab that Bling.

AFTER A FASHION

So what's *Infinity Nikki* like? Imagine the fashion side quests in *Tears of the Kingdom* were the center of the entire game and you're getting there!

MIRA IMAGE

Previous *Nikki* games were presented like visual novels, but now there's an open world to explore. Stylist Nikki and her cat Momo have been sucked into Miraland (Mirror Land, you see?).

COZY WITH A CORE OF DRAMA

Infinity Nikki sells itself as "the coziest open-world game," but it's not all softball stuff—there is combat, and a looming threat Nikki has to resolve. At the outset, she's tasked with finding why residents of Florawish have been slipping into comas.

LORE GIVERS

With greater scale comes deeper lore. Here in Miraland, fashion is worshipped alongside gods! It's a lot to take in at first, but there are lore books scattered around to give you valuable background.

SNAP IT UP

You can enjoy the game without really doing anything! Just wander around and use the photo mode to grab images of yourself wearing favorite outfits in spectacular locations.

FAST FACT

***Infinity Nikki* is released by Chinese company Infold, who are also responsible for the sci-fi romance game *Love and Deepspace*. Following *Infinity Nikki*, they've made further moves into the freemium RPG world with the more action-based *Ballad of Antara*.**

LIKE THIS? TRY THIS:

STYLE SAVVY: STYLING STAR

This Nintendo 3DS game has more depth and smarter design than other dress-up games. You run a boutique and earn money by being good at designing what your customers want!

ŌKAMI:
THE CLASSIC THAT FLOPPED

WE'RE NOT CRYING WOLF—ŌKAMI IS BACK!

Games companies always use the run-up to the Game Awards to announce new projects, and in 2024 the announcement that got everyone talking was a sequel to a game from 2006 that you might not have heard of.

Ōkami was made for the PlayStation 2, which had one of the biggest user bases of any console in history. It got incredible reviews—and yet it sold poorly. So how did it happen?

LUCKY STARS

■ By the early 2000s, Capcom was one of the world's leading game developers. Its hit series included *Mega Man* and *Street Fighter*, and it was working on the first *Monster Hunter* game. It set up a studio within the company called Clover Studio, with the aim of producing original games to stand alongside its ongoing franchises.

One of the staff members assigned to the new studio was Hideki Kamiya, whose previous games had been very well received, so expectations were high for his first game for Clover.

WANDERING WOLF

Some of the biggest games to come out of Japan, such as *Pokémon* and *Zelda*, have sought to give players the experience of exploring the natural world. Kamiya was keen to create something similar, applying realistic graphics to something lighter.

"The only starting point we had for *Ōkami* was a game that depicted a lot of nature," he told *Famitsu* in 2009. "We made this minute-long video depicting a wolf running through a field and trees sprouting up behind him." But Kamiya hadn't considered what the actual gameplay would involve: "Our first test run was incredibly boring to play," he said.

Kamiya is a huge *Zelda* fan, and this influenced how the game developed. The team brought in tales from Japanese folklore about Amaterasu, the Shinto sun goddess who took the form of a white wolf, and is said to have saved the land from darkness.

BRUSHING UP

Although Kamiya initially wanted the game to have realistic graphics, this was putting a strain on the PS2. Character designer Kenichiro Yoshimura experimented by drawing a new Amaterasu with a brush, and this was adopted as the style for the whole game. According to studio head Atsushi Inaba, this led them to ask "Wouldn't it be great if we could somehow get the player involved and participate in this artwork instead of just watching it?"

This was how the team created the Celestial Brush. When the game was paused, the player could bring up a canvas and paint onto it. This was very challenging to implement but became an interface for combat, puzzles, and more.

"At the risk of sounding pretentious, I would like people to feel an overwhelming feeling of beauty when they play it," Inaba said when the game launched.

"IT TAKES ALL THE BEST BITS OF *ZELDA* (THE STRUCTURE, ATMOSPHERE, PUZZLES), THROWS IN WONDERFULLY ORIGINAL COMBAT AND THE MOST ADORABLE ART STYLE EVER SEEN IN A VIDEOGAME . . . IT REALLY IS AN EXCEPTIONAL ACHIEVEMENT ON SO MANY LEVELS."

KRISTAN REED, *EUROGAMER*

FAILURE TO LAUNCH

Ōkami was released to glowing reviews and topped several lists of the best games of 2006. However, its sales were disappointing by Capcom's standards. The *Guinness World Records: Gamer's Edition* named it the lowest-selling winner of a major Game of the Year award.

Less than a year after *Ōkami* was released, Capcom closed Clover Studio. Kamiya, along with *Ōkami*'s producer Atsushi Inaba, and Shinji Mikami had already decided to leave and form their own company, SEEDS Inc.—which soon merged with another company to form PlatinumGames.

A LONG AFTERLIFE

Ōkami quietly lived on. First it was released on the Wii, then in 2012 an HD port of the game came out on the PS3. This was later released for PS4, Xbox One, and Switch. Sales of the PS2 original only totaled a few hundred thousand, but with the HD versions, its reputation grew and grew. It has now sold more than 4.2 million copies!

Even so, the biggest *Ōkami* fans must have given up on ever seeing a sequel. But in 2020, Ikumi Nakamura said she was going to approach Capcom about a new game in the series, and insist Kamiya was involved. Kamiya left PlatinumGames in 2023, and his contract stated he couldn't make any new games for a year—but as soon as that expired, he became head of a new studio called Clovers, which made an *Ōkami* sequel their first project.

"*Ōkami* sequel project is underway," said the announcement. "*Ōkami* is a game critically acclaimed for its unique world, heartwarming story, and exciting adventures. Now, a new adventure in the same vein as *Ōkami* has been set in motion."

It's going to be a while before we get to see it. But it should be something special!

ŌKAMIDEN

Many players suggested *Ōkami's* brush mechanic made it ideal for the DS—but instead of a straight port or sequel, the DS got a "spiritual successor" game called *Ōkamiden*, which was made by a different team from the original. You play as Amaterasu's son Chibiterasu and must find and defeat the evil Akuro, who has placed a curse on the land. While *Ōkamiden* didn't get the ecstatic reviews of *Ōkami*, it was generally regarded as a worthwhile follow-up.

Botany Manor

A game about plants that really grows on you!

Not so long ago, most video games involved you playing as a guy who punches people, a guy who shoots people, or a guy who jumps on people's heads. But games offer a lot more variety these days, which means now you get to play as a retired botanist who lives in a big house in Victorian England!

The cozy genre has become a big part of the gaming world, and *Botany Manor* certainly belongs in that category. But where some cozy games lack much of a challenge, leaving you wandering aimlessly in a nicely designed world, this game has plenty going on!

In a casual manor

The main character, Arabella Greene, has inherited the sprawling Botany Manor, where she intends to continue her research into rare plants. It's a low-key magical world where plants can do stuff they can't do in reality.

FAST FACT

***Botany Manor* is the first game by Balloon Studios, founded by Laure De Mey, who is also the creative lead on this game. Her previous credits include *Alba: A Wildlife Adventure* and *Desta: The Memories Between*.**

Green fingers

■ The vibe is similar to the eerie puzzle game *The Witness*. You're all alone in this large house, with puzzles everywhere—but they take the form of plants. You need to work out what needs to be done to make each plant grow.

Face-plant

■ The information you need will be there—you just need to find it. The puzzles get complicated and may leave you stumped at times, but if you do resort to looking up solutions online, you won't be left wondering how you were meant to work *that* out.

On another note

■ It's not a particularly long game, but there's so much to hold in your head, you'd probably get confused if it went on much longer. It's worth keeping your own notebook for writing down things, like the details of clues, as the in-game book only records their location.

Opportunities for growth

■ Along the way, *Botany Manor* even engages with serious real-world issues, such as Arabella's difficulties as a female academic in the Victorian era. The vibe may be cozy, but this is a game that challenges you in multiple ways!

SAND LAND

A GAME THAT LEAVES YOU THIRSTY FOR MORE!

Sand Land is one of the lesser known works by manga artist Akira Toriyama, creator of *Dragon Ball*. (When you created the bestselling manga of all time, all your other works are lesser known.) It is set in a future where water has become scarce, and Sheriff Rao has rebelled against his greedy King to join forces with the demon prince Beelzebub and his friend Thief, in search of a new source of water.

Toriyama also worked in the games industry, designing characters for *Chrono Trigger* and *Dragon Quest*, and the *Sand Land* game was one of the last projects he worked on before his death in 2024. But how does this short, light manga translate to a big, open-world action RPG?

QUICK TIPS

TUNE IN

Each region has two radio towers. Make it your priority to locate and repair the towers in each region as you enter it, as this saves you filling in the map.

HOARD EARLY, HOARD OFTEN

Collect as much loot as you can early on—there are optional loot sources during the Head to the Legendary Spring mission. You can then be ready with loot to pay for vehicle upgrades when available.

MOVE IT

When in the battle tank, your nitro is like a dodge button in a fighting game. Use it in very quick bursts to evade enemy attacks, because it overheats!

INTO THE SANDBOX

The first thing that strikes you about this game is how well it combines 3D graphics with a 2D manga look. The textures appear drawn but move like they're real. It's odd, but effective!

DRIVING YOU WILD

Instead of Rao, you play as Beelzebub—but actually you spend much of your time steering vehicles and controlling robots, and this is where the real fun of the game lies.

MECH A MOVE

Building and customizing your mechs and vehicles is so enjoyable, and you really feel ownership over your collection. It can be difficult to choose which mechs to carry with you!

STRIKING OUT IN A NEW DIRECTION

The opening sections may seem like standard RPG fare, but work through them, and you'll be rewarded with new vehicle types and abilities. Fans of the manga will also notice some changes to the story…

TREE-MENDOUS

The game really opens out and explores the *Sand Land* world—it even includes a location called Forest Land, created by Toriyama for the anime released in 2024.

FAST FACT

The *Sand Land* manga was published in *Weekly Shōnen Jump* in 2000. In contrast to the epic length of *Dragon Ball*, the whole series is collected in one book, so it's not a big commitment!

LIKE THIS? TRY THIS:

WORLD OF TANKS

If *Sand Land* whets your appetite for more tank-based action, *World of Tanks* offers free online tank battles on demand. Over 600 models of tank from across the twentieth century are available!

SKILLS AND UPGRADES

Sand Land uses skill trees that you can spend points on. The main skill tree is Beelzebub's, but each of his three allies have their own, smaller skill trees that enhance the support they give you. Here's what to unlock first for each character and for the different vehicle types!

BEELZEBUB

The best skills to unlock first for Beelzebub are New Finishing Move, Brace for Attack, Sweeping Attack, Enhance Weak Attack, Aerial Evasion, Charged Attack, Max HP Boost 1, and Enhance Powerful Attack. This lot will cost you 10 skill points. Aerial Evasion is particularly helpful when entering facilities, because you'll be attacked by bots from the air, and having a charged attack is generally very useful.

RAO

Rao's best skill is Vehicular Warfare, which means he assists you during battles by summoning his tank. Unlock this and get the upgrade, too. It's also worth getting Tonfa Attack, which allows Rao to intercept enemies.

ANN

Fuel Saver+ gives you a brief moment where boost costs no energy! As well as this, Ann's Vehicle Recovery+ is valuable, enhancing vehicles' recovery Items.

THIEF

Thief's role in battle is to increase the amount of loot you grab. He does have one offensive skill, though—Boom Box, where he throws a bomb at enemies—so unlock it and make sure he's got something to fight with. Spoils of War and Pilfering Pro both increase the chance of enemies dropping items.

VEHICLES

■ With the Tank, you should first aim to upgrade the Tank Gun, and equip the Gatling Gun+ or Heavy Machine Gun as soon as you get it. With the Jump Bot, unlock the EX Chip and boost endurance and/or recovery. The Motorbike benefits from Flaming Boost and better suspension: The Hovercar should also get a suspension upgrade, as well as the engine. With the Battle Armor, upgrade the Brass Knuckle Arm and unlock the EX Chip.

FAST FACT

The developer of *Sand Land*, ILCA, has experience adapting manga into RPGs—they made 2023's *One Piece Odyssey*. They also created the Switch remakes of *Pokémon Diamond* and *Pearl*.

MIX IT UP

■ It's good to build a collection of vehicles with a wide array of attacks, because you can switch between them during a fight (and you'll want to anyway if one gets badly damaged). Different enemies have different weak points, so go into battle with a variety of weapons.

TOP 10 METROIDVANIA GAMES

Explore, upgrade, and break down barriers!

Metroidvania is a hugely popular genre, especially in the indie world. If you don't know what it actually is, the name comes from two classic series that began in the 1980s—*Metroid* and *Castlevania* (you might have worked that out). It means a type of adventure game where the player explores a large map with areas they can't access until they've found particular items, upgrades, or information—so instead of going from one end of a level to the other, you expand the world outward.

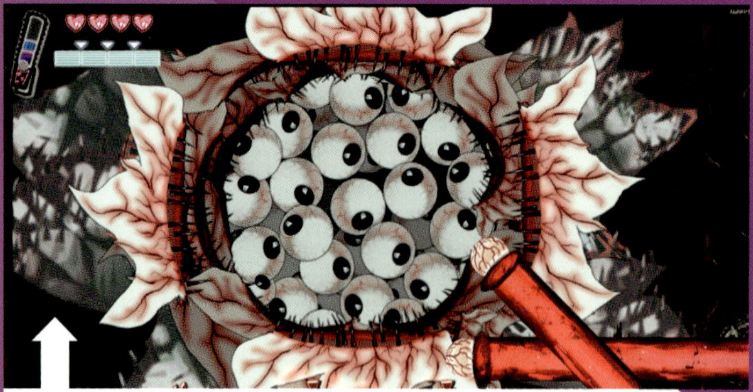

10 The Weird Dream

It feels a bit on-the-nose to put the word "weird" in the title of a video game, and potentially disappointing: What if it's not actually that weird? But this is pretty surreal stuff, and while it's not doing anything groundbreaking, it's well put together, with an open design that lets you find your own path.

AVAILABLE ON: PC

09 Mira and the Legend of the Djinns

The indie scene is producing more and more titles that come from a different cultural background to the ones usually represented in gaming. *Mira and the Legend of the Djinns* is rooted in Moroccan and Amazigh mythology. The game takes you across deserts and through crumbling deserted cities in search of the secret of the last Djinn.

AVAILABLE ON: PC

08 Bō: Path of the Teal Lotus

■ A lighter take on Metroidvania with more linear progression, *Bō: Path of the Teal Lotus* stands out for its incredible hand-drawn graphics, inspired by Japanese mythology and the country's tradition of woodblock prints. The Japanese cultural references extend to the gameplay: As the hero Bō fights enemies, his kettle fills with tea, which he can use to recharge his health.

AVAILABLE ON: **Nintendo Switch, PS5, Xbox Series S/X, PC**

07 Caravan SandWitch

■ A lot of Metroidvanias are frantic and tricky, with death waiting around every corner. *Caravan SandWitch* is more relaxed, with quests that aren't too challenging and put the emphasis on exploring at your own pace and in your own way. You play as Sauge, a young woman who's driving around her home planet in a van, searching for her missing sister.

AVAILABLE ON: **Nintendo Switch, PS5, PC**

06 Tevi

■ The titular Tevi is helping out with her father's research by hunting for Astral Gears, which are a powerful source of an energy called mana. She is accompanied by an angel called Celia and a demon called Sable, who follow her inside floating orbs. This is an accessible steampunk take on Metroidvania, with lots of adjustable settings so you can set it up for speedrunning or to provide a bigger challenge, and multiple goals in each area so you can leave the trickier parts until later.

AVAILABLE ON: **Nintendo Switch, PS5, Xbox Series S/X, Xbox One, PC**

05 Voidwrought

■ Excellent hand-drawn graphics and atmospheric music enhance this well-designed, *Hollow Knight*–influenced Metroidvania in which you explore the ruins of an ancient civilization. It's light on story but heavy on lore, and lots of the enjoyment lies in looking out for the visual evidence of the world that came before. It also throws in some interesting combat mechanics, such as the way you dodge back immediately before striking a blow: Once you get used to this, it's great for evading damage.

AVAILABLE ON:
Nintendo Switch, PC

04 Frontier Hunter: Erza's Wheel of Fortune

■ Erza previously appeared in the 2019 roguelite game *Tower Hunter: Erza's Trial*, where she was trying to acquire her Hunter's License. Now she's got it, but her spaceship has broken down on a hostile planet with only a sentient quipping hairpin called Diablo for company. This anime-style adventure looks great and plays very smoothly, with a combat system that encourages strategy and thought rather than just leaping in and smashing your sword around.

AVAILABLE ON:
PS5, PC, Mac

03 Ultros

■ This is like a more surreal take on *Metroid*. You play as Ouji, a sort of humanoid insect: She's crash-landed into a giant mysterious spaceship that contains an ancient demon called Ultros. Our heroine must prevent this evil from being unleashed on the universe. *Ultros* has wild, psychedelic visuals—power-ups that take the form of giant eyeball fruit—and the whole thing is just so fascinating, it really draws you in.

AVAILABLE ON:
PS5, PS4, PC, Mac

02 Tales Of Kenzera: ZAU

A lot of recent Metroidvanias are cleverly designed but the story is nothing remarkable. *Tales of Kenzera: ZAU*, however, has it all—perfectly entertaining combat and exploration attached to superb, emotionally rich storytelling. Its Afrofuturist world is brilliantly brought to life, and it deals with weighty themes of grief as shaman Zau tries to deliver three spirits to the god of death so he can bring his father back to life. It's quite the journey!

AVAILABLE ON:
Nintendo Switch, PS5, Xbox S/X, PC

01 Rusted Moss

In this fantasy adventure you play as Fern, a changeling caught in the middle of the war between humans and fae folk. The iron weapons used by humankind to keep the fae at bay are rusting, and the fae are about to get the upper hand. The range of weaponry you can pick up is fascinating, but what really sets *Rusted Moss* apart is its grappling hook, which is the key to opening up new areas of the map, as well as being crucial in boss fights! It's a top-notch take on the genre.

AVAILABLE ON:
Nintendo Switch, PS5, Xbox S/X, PC

STAR WARS OUTLAWS

STEALING STUFF FROM A GALAXY FAR, FAR AWAY

Most *Star Wars* games see you stepping into the role of a Jedi or member of the Rebel Alliance, or even taking control of the Imperial forces. But if you prefer to live the Han Solo life, doing shady business in the back alleys of the Empire and living off your wits, *Outlaws* is the game for you.

It takes place around the time of *The Empire Strikes Back*, so you don't play as Han—he's kind of busy. Instead you are street thief Kay Vess, who escapes a botched heist by stealing a spaceship and crash-landing on a moon called Toshara. A new life as a mercenary begins, as Kay does jobs for various criminal gangs and builds her reputation. It's like *Assassin's Creed* in the *Star Wars* universe!

QUICK TIPS

SABACC IT UP

■ The make-a-pair card game Sabacc is a fun way to boost your money, and you can cheat at it, too. At first, your only option is to send Nix to look at opponents' cards.

DOUBLE DRAW

■ Acquire the Plan A ability by completing the High Roller's quest on Akiva, then you can sneakily draw two cards at once when playing Sabacc.

DICEY MOVE

■ Teeka, the Jawa Hotfixer on Tatooine, can unlock Magnetic Dice for you. This allows you to influence the dice rolls in Sabacc and get an Imposter number that matches your card.

IT ALL MATTERS

Developer Ubisoft has tried to make *Outlaws* as flexible as possible, with consequences for your choices and conversations that can affect later events. The crime syndicates and the Empire may send their minions to take you out!

RETRO FUTURE

The design is immaculate, with lots of references to the movies, and really gives you that *Star Wars* buzz. Even Kay's hair and clothes give her the 1980s-in-space look of the characters in *The Empire Strikes Back*.

TAKE FIVE

You can recruit a crew for your operations, including the battle droid ND-5. The story also has real depth: Kay's connections with others are significant, and we get to see the Rebel Alliance from a different angle.

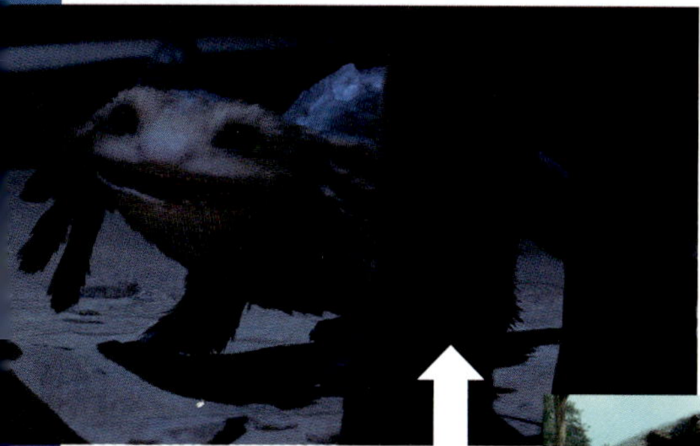

A QUICK NIX

Han had Chewbacca, but Kay has Nix, an axolotl-like creature who follows her around and sometimes sits on her shoulder. Nix can distract guards, fetch items, and crawl into tight spaces for you.

BLAST BUT NOT LEAST

Like Han Solo, Kay believes no weapon is a substitute for a good blaster—so that's the only weapon she keeps hold of. Others can be used until they run out of ammo, but for greater firepower, you need to upgrade the blaster!

FAST FACT

Dee Bradley Baker, who plays ND-5, has been providing voices on animated *Star Wars* productions since the 2008 *Clone Wars* movie. He's played lots of clone troopers and even had a voice role in *The Force Awakens*.

LIKE THIS? TRY THIS:

STAR WARS JEDI: SURVIVOR

If *Outlaws* leaves you wanting to spend some time on the light side of the *Star Wars* universe, this epic sequel to 2019's *Fallen Order* really immerses you in the Jedi way of life!

RISING TO THE TOP IN STAR WARS OUTLAWS

Helping you navigate these wretched hives of scum and villainy.

There's a lot going on in *Outlaws* which means it can be hard to know where to focus your efforts. A key thing to remember is this is a lawless world and many things are possible. For instance, you don't always have to earn everything—often you can steal it!

FAST FACT

***Star Wars Outlaws* was developed by the French software house Ubisoft, which created the *Assassin's Creed* series as well as the recent *Prince of Persia* game *The Lost Crown*.**

1 Expand and contract

■ After completing the quests entitled Underworld, New Tricks, and False Flag, you'll unlock the Contract Brokers. It's a smart idea to prioritize completing the easy contracts. The rewards may be small, but you'll quickly earn a good reputation with the various syndicates, which makes it easier to move around.

2 Unwanted attention

■ At some point you'll get put on the Wanted list, which means more heat from the authorities, but you don't have to just live with it. You can take your name off the list by hacking an Imperial satellite or bribing a corrupt Imperial officer to take it off for you.

3 Creep along

■ As Kay is a thief, there's a lot of stealth involved—and at first this requires patience. So when you get to upgrade your skills and equipment, prioritize stealth—particularly smoke bombs and alarm disabling (alarms are a real killer). Better stealth makes the game less frustrating and speeds things along.

4 Stunning feats

■ Set your blaster to stun when attempting stealth sections. Killing guards will make everything much messier! You can also use your fists—aside from Dark Troopers, droids, and some Gamorreans, you can take enemies down with three melee punches. Alternatively, try the Fast Talk option if you're spotted.

Power snacks

■ Nix's upgrades are unlocked by locating a particular food stall on each planet, paying 200 credits for that stall's Nix Treat, and playing a minigame while Nix eats it. The Toshara stall can be found south of Mirogana Market and gives Nix the ability to repel grenades.

5 Think laterally

■ Bear in mind this isn't a one-route kind of game: There's nearly always more than one way to get in somewhere, and sometimes this will involve using Nix to sabotage alarms, create a distraction, or open vents so you can get a clear shot. Always think about what Nix can be doing.

FIVE NIGHTS AT FREDDY'S: SECRET OF THE MIMIC

Don't open the box! Oh, too late.

It began as a simple point-and-click jump scare game, but over the last decade, *Five Nights at Freddy's* has grown into a multimedia franchise including movies, novels, comics, and tabletop games. It has also developed some pretty twisty lore that still has a lot of unanswered questions, and the eleventh main game in the series, *Secret of the Mimic*, promises to build further on that lore . . .

COPYCAT

■ This game picks up where the DLC for *Five Nights at Freddy's: Security Breach* left off. That DLC—called *Ruin* (rated by many to be superior to the main game)—featured a villain called the Mimic.

FROM THE RUINS

■ In *Ruin*, the Mimic was revealed to be posing as Gregory (the protagonist of *Security Breach*), imitating his voice, and trying to trick a girl named Cassie into deactivating the security protocols to free it.

HIJACKING THE LIMELIGHT

■ Also featured in *Secret of the Mimic* is Jackie, an animatronic based on a jack-in-the-box, who briefly popped up (ho ho) in *Help Wanted 2*. But if you think she's stuck in that box and can't chase you, you're very, very wrong . . .

FAST FACT

Creator Scott Cawthon got the idea for *Five Nights at Freddy's* after players said characters in his game *Chipper & Sons Lumber Co.* looked creepy, which he hadn't intended. He decided to use that style to make the *Freddy* characters creepy on purpose!

WOOLLY THINKING

■ The *FNAF* franchise remains in the hands of developer Steel Wool, which made *Security Breach* as well as the *Help Wanted* games, which were principally made for VR platforms. *Secret of the Mimic* is designed to work for VR and non-VR gamers alike.

ELSIE

Side-Scrolling

Roguelike games, in which levels and enemies are procedurally generated, have a strong fan base, but they can feel repetitive as you blast your way through a seemingly random selection of obstacles. The ones that have done well in recent years, such as *Dead Cells* or *Hades*, have brought in elements of other genres, and have become known as "roguelites." And that is exactly what this game is.

Elsie is a platformer with a similar vibe to the *Mega Man* games. It's set on the planet Ekis, where the title character—a cyborg—is battling her creator's other progeny and trying to locate the missing Guardians in an effort to stop the creatures overrunning the planet. But let's face it, we're not here for the plot—we want action!

QUICK TIPS

ON THE FRONT FOOT

■ Don't be cautious in your approach to *Elsie*—you'll do better by being aggressive and keeping on the move than by finding somewhere safe and picking your moment to attack.

MATCH, DON'T MIX

■ Some of Elsie's abilities work better together than others, so think about how you want to approach a level and pick the abilities that serve that approach.

SPEND SPEND SPEND

■ Don't hoard your currency—everything you buy makes the game easier, so use what you have earned as soon as you get the chance!

QUICK TO CLICK

Elsie is very easy to get the hang of, and it's very quick to blast your way through a level. This feels like a game made for replaying and speedrunning.

RISK AND REWARD

While it's grueling, the game offers regular rewards such as buffs to keep you going, and the gameplay is fast and fun as you attempt to clear each biome—even if the bosses can be a little samey.

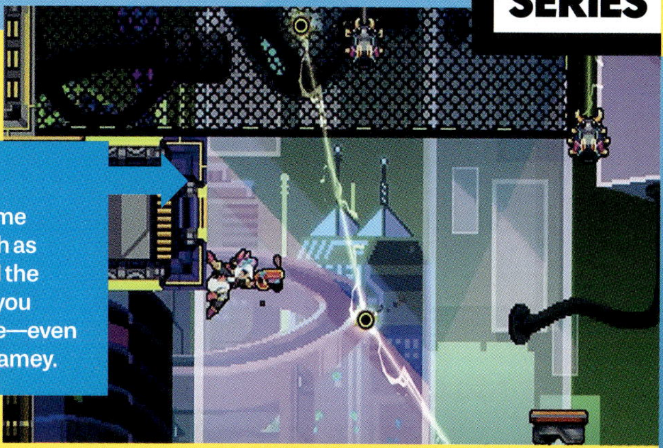

WILD STYLE

Elsie isn't the most original game you'll ever play, but it makes up for this with beautiful design. There's an impressive amount of color and detail in the pixel artwork.

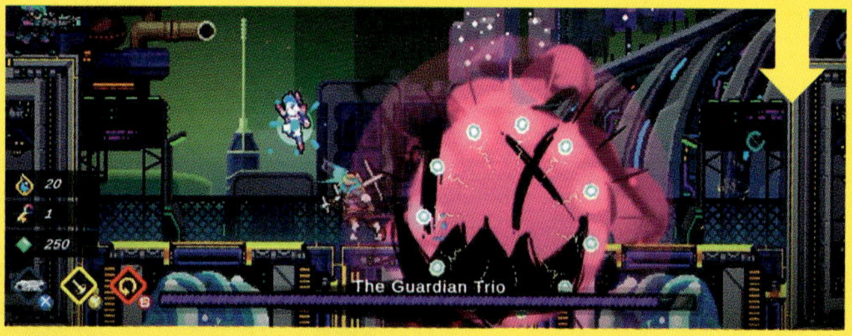

WAVES WASHING OVER YOU

You get subjected to regular arena battles, in which you must fight waves of enemies until they're all vanquished. You can secure blueprints during these encounters that can be used for upgrades.

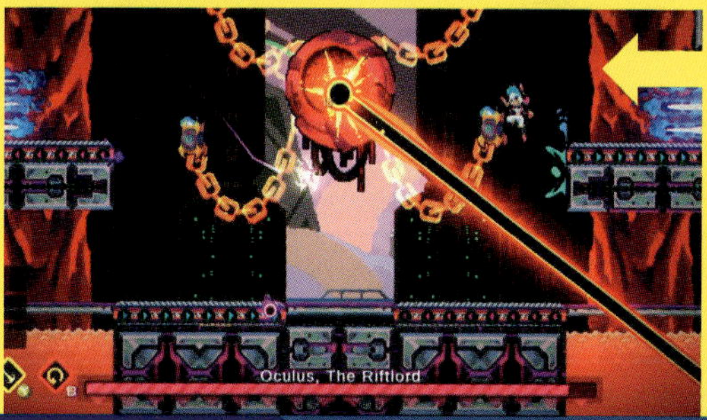

BRIGHT AND BREEZY

Elsie herself packs a lot of personality into a simple little sprite, and praise is also due for the music and animation. The game makes itself an enjoyable experience in every way.

FAST FACT

The accessibility options in *Elsie* include ways to adapt it for those with color blindness—a thoughtful addition in a game that uses color so heavily.

LIKE THIS? TRY THIS:

HADES

One of the best roguelites of recent years, *Hades* is set in the underworld of the dead, so repeatedly dying while trying to escape is all part of the story!

GRANBLUE FANTASY: RELINK

THE MOBILE RPG LINKS UP WITH HOME CONSOLES

Granblue Fantasy started life as a turn-based RPG for phones, but has become so successful, the latest game in the series, *Relink*, has launched on PlayStation and PC. It has been in the works a long time—it was originally scheduled for 2018, and finally appeared in 2024, by which time the fighting spin-off *Granblue Fantasy: Versus* and its sequel, *Rising*, had already appeared on PlayStation and PC, bringing a whole new audience to the series.

You don't need any prior knowledge of the series to pick this game up. The protagonists of *Relink* are a crew of skyfaring explorers searching for the island of Estalucia, where wishes are said to come true. But the path is filled with monsters at every turn—and there are some truly memorable ones!

QUICK TIPS

SPEND WISELY

Sigils can be expensive to upgrade, so don't do it until you've got a Sigil you definitely want to keep. Potion Hoarder and Linked Together are better than they sound!

GREATER GEAR

Leveling up weapons should be your first priority. This is the easiest way to increase your base stats.

RAPID REPEAT

The quest repeat function isn't obvious, but it's handy when you need to go back into a quest—you don't need to go back to town and do it from there.

A SHORTER EPIC

The mobile roots of *Relink* show through in one important way. If you're used to sprawling RPGs that swallow all your gaming time for months, you might be surprised that *Relink*'s main story can be completed in around twenty hours!

DIRECT ACTION

If you feel bogged down when you play long, sprawling RPGs, you may prefer the more direct experience *Relink* offers. It's all about accessibility—you can even automate combat if you would rather just experience the story.

SIMPLICITY AND VARIETY

Combat is done with two buttons, but every fighter plays differently, and it's so smooth you can easily react to what's happening in a battle. This helps prevent combat from getting repetitive.

KEEP IT MOVING

Each chapter has a clear objective and takes place in a new location, and it feels really fast-paced, with a constant stream of action and revelations. There are also side quests if you want them.

GRANBLUE SKIES

The game's anime steampunk stylings are very well rendered, making this a really eye-catching game that makes the most of moving away from pocket-size screens!

FAST FACT

Granblue Fantasy **has also been adapted into an anime, which began in 2017 and ran for two seasons. The comedy short *Grand Blues!* followed in 2020.**

LIKE THIS? TRY THIS:

BASTION

This indie action RPG is a little old now—it came out in 2011—but like *Relink* it's not too long and has got some really smart touches. You may be able to pick it up cheaply, too!

UNDERSTANDING COMBAT IN GRANBLUE FANTASY: RELINK

This excellent system rewards players who use its strengths!

Whereas the original *Granblue Fantasy* used turn-based combat, *Relink* uses real-time action combat. The system is really well designed, and while you're relying on the game's AI to handle the other members of your party, it does a good job of this, so your comrades don't behave in random and mystifying ways. Let's delve into that system a little more!

1

The art of battle

One interesting feature is the Arts level. This rises during battle, with normal attacks adding to the meter. The power of your special skill depends on how high your Arts level is when you unleash it—so the longer you hold off, the more powerful it becomes.

2

Reach for the sky

If you want to deal some serious damage, use the Skybound Arts. Each character has a unique Skybound Attack, and if all members of your party unleash these attacks in sequence, this activates Full Burst. You can instruct your party to save their Skybound Arts if you want them to hold off and use them together.

FAST FACT

Hideo Minaba, the art director of the *Granblue Fantasy* games, previously worked on the *Final Fantasy* series: He was one of the main artists on the acclaimed *Final Fantasy VI*.

3 Make links

The Link system is perhaps the most important thing to focus on. The blue bar above an enemy's head is their Stun Gauge, and when it's broken, you have a chance to make a Link Attack. This charges another meter—your Link level. When it's at 100 percent, make another attack…

4 Take your time

…and enter Link Time. Cooldowns are reduced, attacks are stronger, and time around your party slows down. Get used to using this strategy early in the game, because when you face off against tougher enemies later, Link Time can make all the difference!

In their element

As you recruit new characters, you get more options for mixing up your party. Often, a character who can provide healing support and/or a tank to absorb damage is a good addition, and if you can assemble a party with the same elements, this will help against particular bosses. Switch up your party if you're struggling to get past a fight.

5 Make it perfect

After upgrading your Defense Mastery, you can make Perfect Blocks and Dodges. If you're struggling to execute Perfect Dodges, try dodging into the danger instead of away from it. This may seem weirdly wrong, but it does give a better chance of a Perfect Dodge and a brief spell of invincibility.

Animal Well

Well, that's pretty wild.

■ *Animal Well* is a Metroidvania without combat. Instead it offers a series of puzzles, the first of which is "What is even going on here?" Its blobby protagonist hatches from a flower at the start of the game, after which you're given zero backstory, no clue what you're meant to be doing, and very little in the way of prompts. You may have guessed from the title that you're trapped in a well that's full of animals—but the rest . . . Well, we'll let you work out for yourself. You may think you've played games like this before, but trust us, you haven't!

Well lit

■ At first glance you might think this isn't anything special: Its pixel graphics look OK, but there are plenty of games that look like this. But the animation is great, and the dim neon light creates an amazing atmosphere.

Hoard to progress

Many Metroidvanias have an RPG-like quality, where your character needs to become more powerful to access other areas of the map and to cope with what they find there. *Animal Well* isn't like that: You never get more powerful, but you do accumulate stuff.

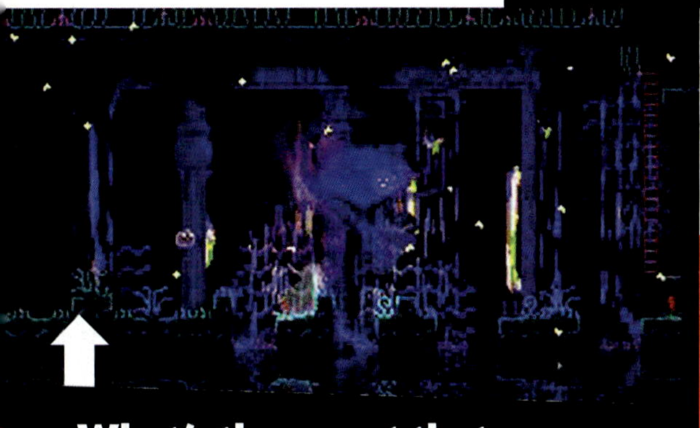

Touch type

And here's a bonus—if you buy this on Switch and play in handheld mode, you can interact with the game via the touchscreen! So few games make use of this feature, you can easily forget it's there.

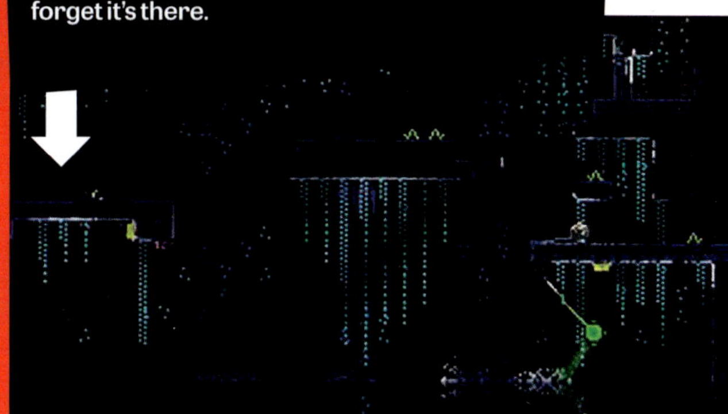

What's the worst that can happen?

The key to progress is to experiment. Play around with the items you find, see if you can use them in combination with one another, and use what you've learned about the world as you tackle each new area.

FAST FACT

***Animal Well* was designed and built by Billy Basso, who spent seven years creating it. He built a new game engine for it, feeling the off-the-shelf engines were bloated and inefficient.**

Hidden depths

Bear in mind, every screen has something hidden in it somewhere—maybe more than one something! So, while it's not a particularly long game—you can get through it in about six hours—you can easily sink a lot more time into finding all its secrets.

GLOSSARY

Achievement
An award added to your online profile for completing goals or objectives in a game.

AI
Artificial intelligence. Intelligent behavior simulated by a computer to, for instance, control how enemies behave toward a player, or control other players on your team in a sports game.

Backward compatible
A console that can play games originally designed for older platforms.

Battle royale
A type of action game where sixty or more players are dropped onto a single large map and fight until just one survives.

Boss
A bigger, tougher enemy that players have to fight at the end of a level or mission in a game.

Campaign
A series of levels or objectives connected by some kind of story, usually making up the single-player mode of a game.

Sid Meier's Civilization VII

CCG
Collectible card game. A style of game based on real-world card games, where players collect an army of cards and use them to battle other players.

Checkpoint
A point in a game where your progress is saved. If you die, you'll return to the checkpoint.

City building
A type of simulation game in which a player builds and governs their own city.

Combo
In a fighting game or action game, a series of button presses that triggers a hard-hitting attack or counterattack.

Co-op
A game or game mode where players can work together to complete objectives or win the game.

Crafting
Using materials collected within a game to make useful items, armor, or weapons.

Cutscene
An animated sequence or video sequence in a game, used to build atmosphere or tell the story.

DLC
Downloadable content. Additional items, characters, or levels for a game that you can buy and download as extras.

Pocket Bravery

FPS
First-person shooter. A style of game where players move around a map, shooting enemies from a first-person perspective, with a view straight from the hero's eyes.

Grind
To play through an area or section of a game over and over again to harvest loot or collect experience points and level up.

Hub
The central area within a video game that a player frequently returns to to access different game levels.

Indie game
Short for independent. A game created by a small team of developers—or even a single developer.

Penny's Big Breakaway

JRPG

Japanese role-playing game. A Japanese-made, role-playing game with the kind of gameplay and graphics you'd expect from a *Final Fantasy*, *Persona*, or *Dragon Quest* game.

Level

A portion or chapter of a game set in one area and with a beginning, an end, and a series of goals and challenges in between.

Life simulation

A type of simulation game that emulates real-life. Players control the lives of humans, animals, or other living things and make choices to shape their destiny.

Map

An in-game map to help you find objectives, or a level where players can fight in a multiplayer game.

Metroidvania

A type of action-adventure game that emphasizes free exploration rather than straightforward progression.

Microtransactions

Small purchases made within a video game. They can enhance the gaming experience and are a feature in many free-to-play games.

NPC

Non-player character. A character in a game controlled by the computer. NPCs often provide help or guidance, sell goods, or help tell the story of the game.

Promenade

Open world

A style of game where players are free to explore one or more large areas and try out different activities, rather than complete one level after another.

Platformer

Platform game. A type of game where you run across a series of platforms or a challenging landscape, leaping over gaps and obstacles, and avoiding or defeating enemies in your path.

Port

A version of a game made for one console or computer that's been converted to run on another.

Retro

A game or visual style that looks back to older games from the 1980s or 1990s.

Roguelike

A style of game where players fight through a series of randomly generated levels, killing monsters and collecting weapons and equipment.

RPG

Role-playing game. A type of game where the player goes on an epic quest or adventure, fighting monsters, leveling up, and upgrading their equipment along the way.

Season pass

An add-on for a game that allows you to download and play through any expansions or DLC released after it launches.

Shoot-'em-up

A style of game based on classic arcade games, where players work their way through waves of levels full of enemies, blasting away at them and avoiding their attacks.

Cataclismo

Speedrun

A gaming challenge where players compete to finish a game or level in the shortest possible time.

Streaming

Watching a video or playing a game through a live connection to the internet, rather than downloading it and then playing it from a console or computer.

VR

Virtual reality. Playing games through a head-mounted screen with motion controls, so that it looks and feels more like you're actually in the game world.

XP

Experience points. Points scored in a game for completing objectives, beating challenges, or killing monsters, and often used to upgrade the hero, their skills, or their equipment.

Sonic X Shadow Generations